Scintillating Portals into the Fantastic

The Art of

James William Christenson

Kayto & Co. Publishing

Minneapolis | Minnesota | USA

Scintillating Portals into the Fantastic

The Art of James William Christenson

8860 154th St W
Prior Lake, Minnesota, 55372, USA
jim@jamesartstudio.com
www.jamesartstudio.com

ISBN-13: 978-1-7327129-9-7
ISBN-10: 1-7327129-9-9
Library of Congress Control Number: 2019915049

Kayto & Co. Publishing
Minneapolis, Minnesota, USA
Editor: Jason J. Christenson

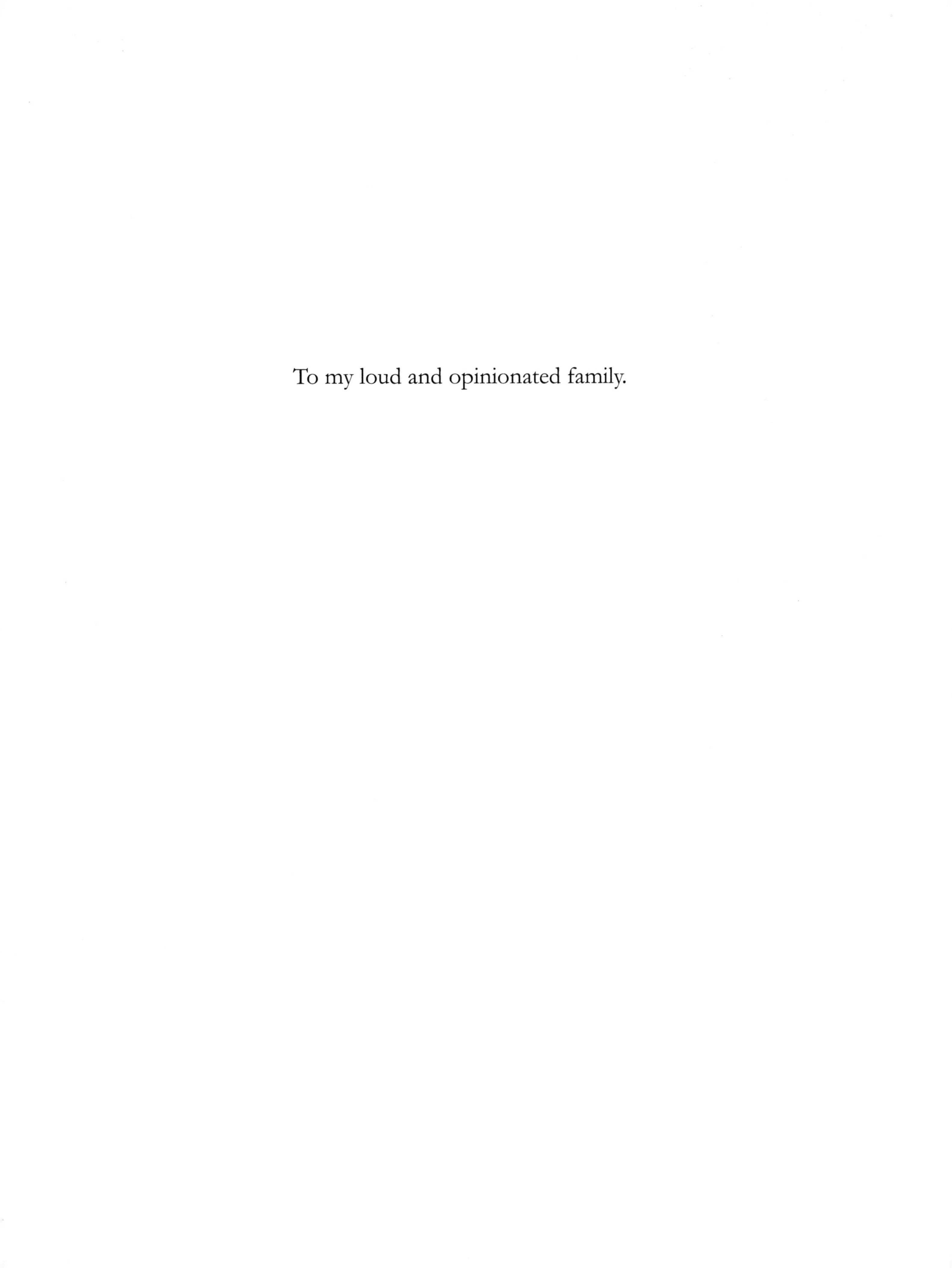

To my loud and opinionated family.

Artist Note

As a young child, I set my sights on being an elephant - not an artist. Although I was artistically inclined, being an elephant seemed to be the best choice of a profession for me since elephants were my favorite animal. At one point, I even asked my pediatric dentist if my tusks were coming in. Now that I understand that elephants are paid peanuts and I can receive the same wage as an artist without sacrificing my rugged good looks, I am pursuing a career in art. However, much of my art still reflects my love of the pachyderm.

I can't remember a time when I was without a pencil, pen, brush, or lump of clay. When I was three years old, I constructed a three-dimensional paper replica of my brother's graduation cap, tassel included. My parents were so impressed that they topped his cake with it. Ever since then, I've been creating for the enjoyment of others from my own pleasurable memories and imagination.

When I was about eight years old, I illustrated a book that I was writing. My art included dragons, monsters, villains, and heroes. It lacked the one thing that I was least interested in drawing: damsels in distress. My sister insisted upon a heroine and demanded that I add a female character, thus expanding my portraiture portfolio.

Around the age of twelve, I began a more serious pursuit of the craft, believing that I could actually make my way in the world doing the thing that I loved best. I started art lessons from Patricia Schwartz, whose realism, attention to detail, skill and knowledge I admired, respected and coveted. Around the same time, I began an online art class from Sharon Hofer, who influenced my experimentation in different mediums including wood, rice paper, clay, pastels, stained glass, mosaics, colored pencil, gouache, and others. Chad Steward, a former Disney animator, taught me animation skills and helped me develop an entire animated film, giving me a deeper appreciation for the old hand-drawn classic Disney movies.

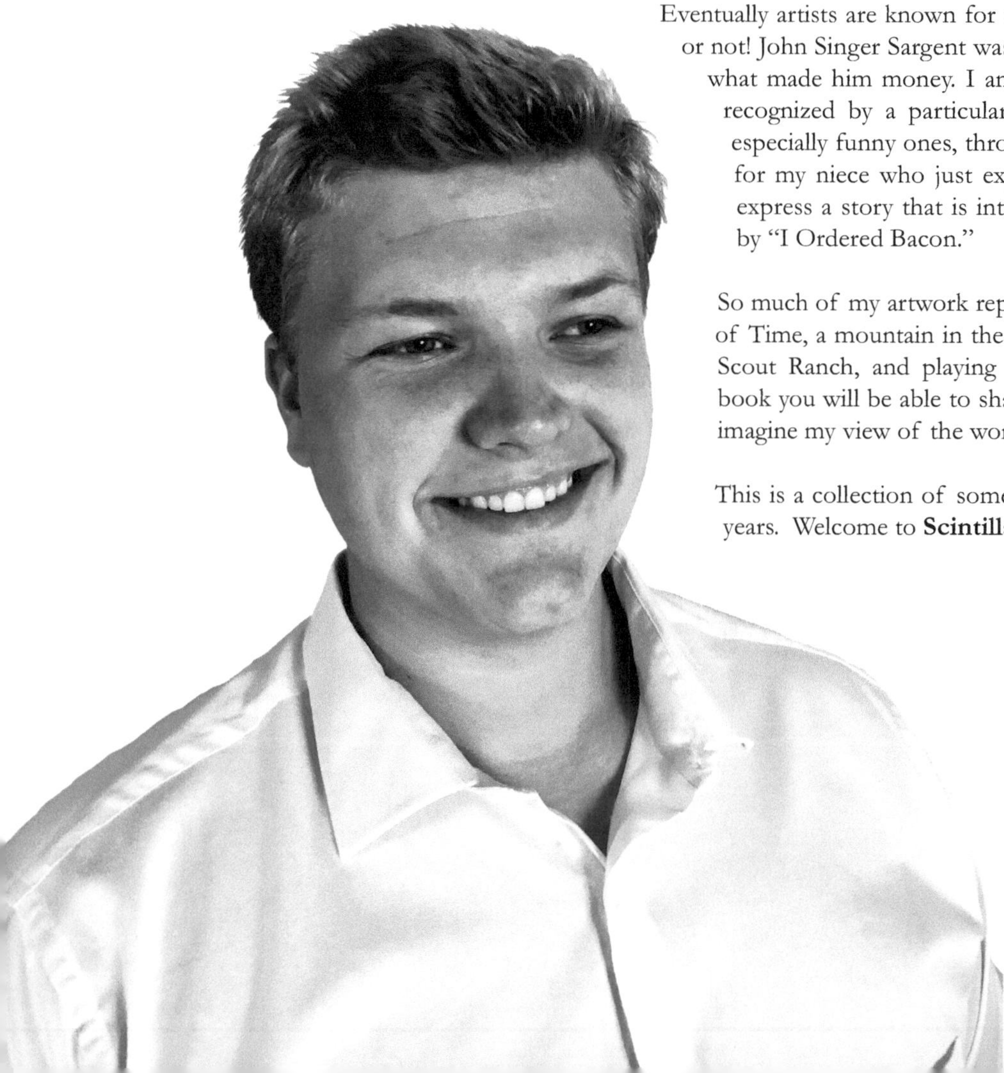

Eventually artists are known for a particular medium or style - whether they like it or not! John Singer Sargent was known for his oil portraits. That's what sold and what made him money. I am still developing my style and am not tied to or recognized by a particular medium or subject yet. I enjoy telling stories, especially funny ones, through my artwork as in the piece "Eleanor," named for my niece who just experienced her first lemon. Most of my cartoons express a story that is intended to generate a giggle like the one generated by "I Ordered Bacon."

So much of my artwork represent my best memories, like climbing the Tooth of Time, a mountain in the New Mexico Rocky Mountain range at Philmont Scout Ranch, and playing cards with family and friends. Throughout this book you will be able to share in some of these memories, chuckle a bit, and imagine my view of the world as you enter into my art.

This is a collection of some of my favorite pieces that I have made over the years. Welcome to **Scintillating Portals into the Fantastic**.

Cordially,

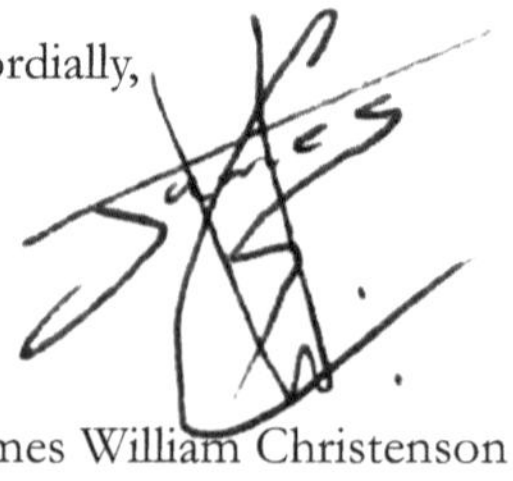

James William Christenson

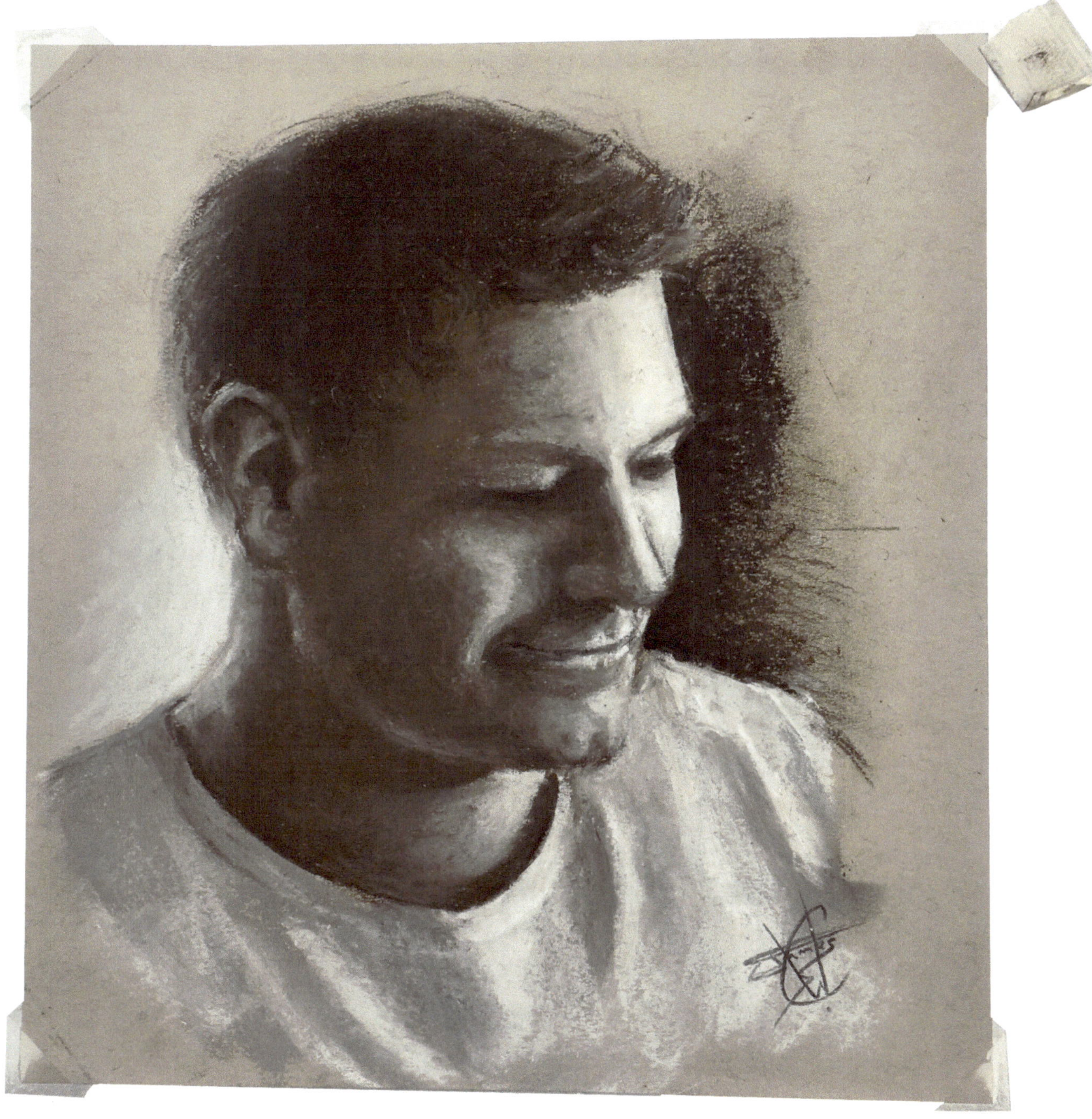

"Self Portrait"
2018

Paper
Pastel

9.0 L × 8.0 W Inches

In the Archives of the James William Christenson Art Gallery, Prior Lake, Minnesota

Introduction

There is a subtle and meaningful difference between buying and collecting art. Superficially, art collectors and art buyers perform the same activities: Both acquire art representative of particular tastes, preferences, colorations, media, and subject matters. The consequential difference between art buyers and art collectors is in the approach. Buying artwork is a transactional task. Collecting artwork is a purposeful, long-term commitment to researching, evaluating, and forming a meaningful grouping of artwork around a specific set of criteria.

Given this philosophy, Casa de Flamingo's decision to include James William's art in its collection is an interesting one. James William's incredible diversity in media, subject matter, and stylistic approach can be described as a complete absence of commonality, making any collection of his work a seemingly non-traditional affair. Nevertheless, there is a commonality to his work after all. An often understated humor and a deeply ironic juxtaposition can be found in nearly all of his works. His painting "Uncropped Vermeer" is certainly one of the most obvious and unconventional pieces in this collection that characterize this element. In fact, most of his pieces feature creatures, people, or things that evoke a range of emotions but are nuanced and layered for levels of enjoyment, education, and consumption.

Take, for instance, some of the examples of James William's "Deck of Cards" series contained herein. Ostensibly, these cards depict traditional playing card figures from the face cards, while the inverse image depicts a re-imagined grotesque or medieval character and related themes. There are different surprises as rewards for the attentive. A casual observer will doubtless note the detail of the characters, thematic approach for each suit with animals or weaponry, and color variations, too. Upon a deeper inspection, however, observation might reveal that the "hearts" suit cards all feature an anatomical heart or that "diamond" cards depict a diamond gemstone somewhere. A very close inspection will reveal, buried deep in the details, a pastry, like a croissant, muffin, or donut. The incongruence between the innocence of playing cards, gnarly motifs, and hidden pastries highlights the fascinating elements that make James William's work so engaging.

> The real enjoyment of James William's work is sharing it with others and watching their reactions or depth of observation.

Other pieces of his work are more subtle. On an eighty-mile backpacking trip in the New Mexican high desert of the Rocky Mountain range, he took hundreds of pictures of the scenery, including the original panoramic photo that inspired his work, entitled, "Three Mountain Top Experiences." This wonderful landscape scene from the top of a mountain captures the moment shortly after summiting the peak and depicts three members of his backpacking crew. One is bent over, exhausted, little caring for the achievement or beauty of the movement, another is serenely taking in the breathtaking scene around him, almost in a meditative state, and the third is oblivious to the world and the incredible scenery around him - he is relieving himself. The painting is as much about the landscape and story as it is a joke on his audience!

Most pieces of artwork in this collection tell a story and are certainly interesting in their own right, but the real delight with James William's work is sharing it with others and watching their reactions or depth of observation. This multilayered and shared amusement is gives deeper experiential depth to James William's work.

I hope you enjoy the selected works enclosed in these pages. Many of these pieces have not been publicly displayed before. Look through it - closely - then share what you have discovered with others to continue the amusement and story. James William's art showcased in **Scintillating Portals into the Fantastic** will certainly not disappoint!

Enjoy!

Jason J. Christenson
Curator, **Casa de Flamingo**

"Uncropped Vermeer"
2019

Stretched Canvas Over Wooden Frame
Oil
19.0 L × 24.0 W Inches

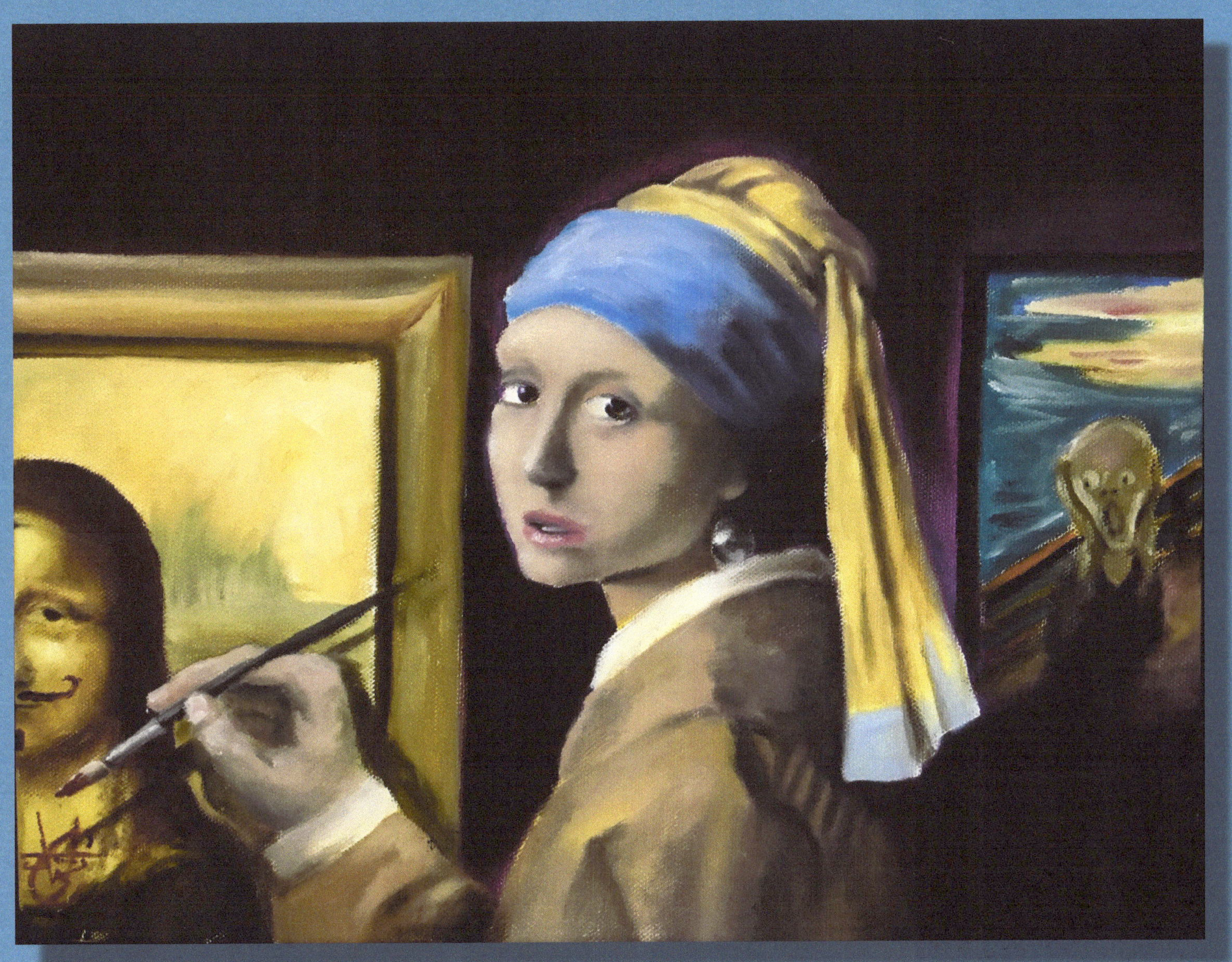

On Loan. The Private Art Collection of Casa de Flamingo, Minnesota

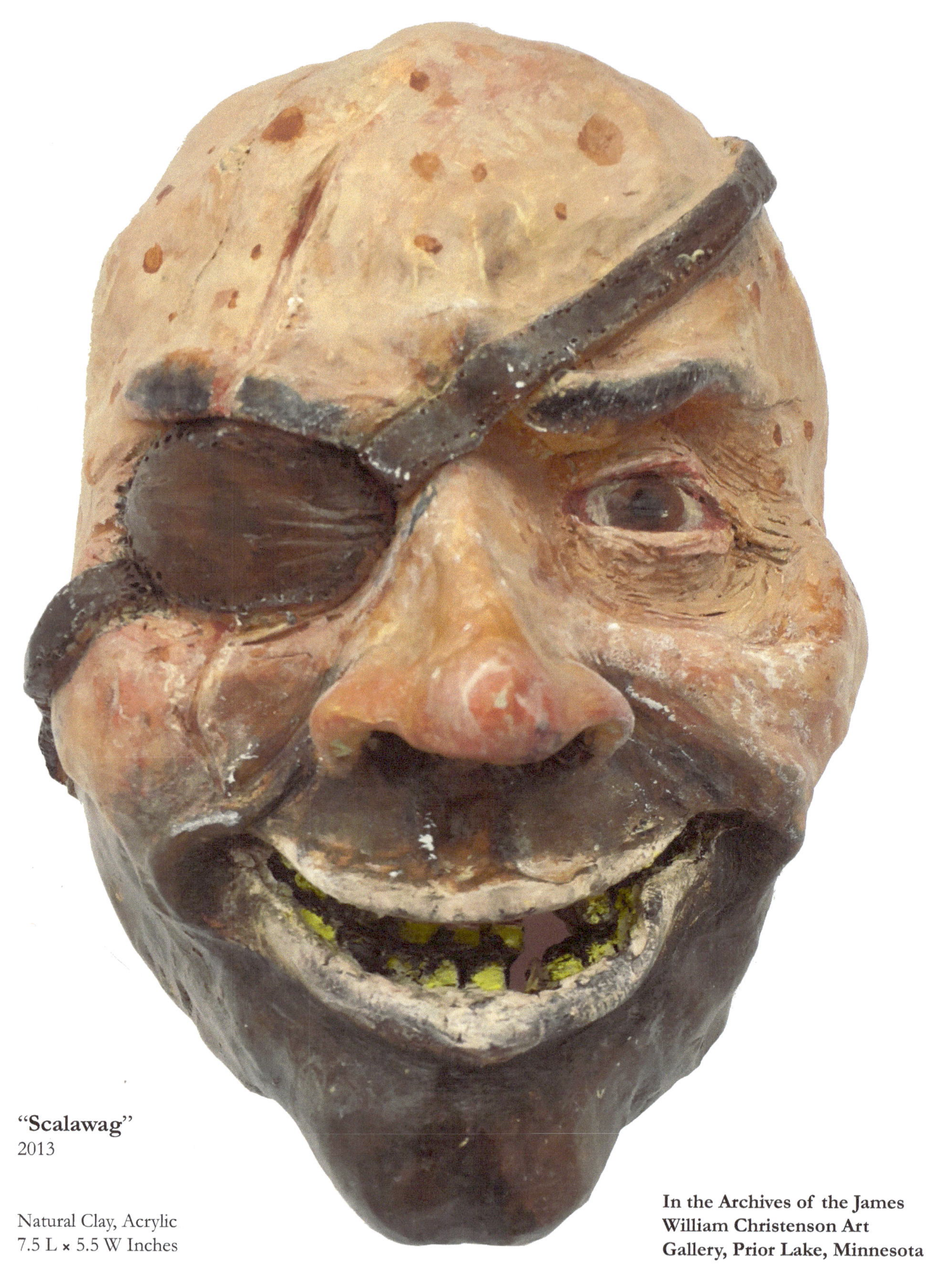

"Scalawag"
2013

Natural Clay, Acrylic
7.5 L × 5.5 W Inches

In the Archives of the James William Christenson Art Gallery, Prior Lake, Minnesota

"Hadji Ali's Tomb"
2018

Cardstock
Pencil, Felt Pen, Ink, Acrylic

7.0 L × 5.0 W Inches

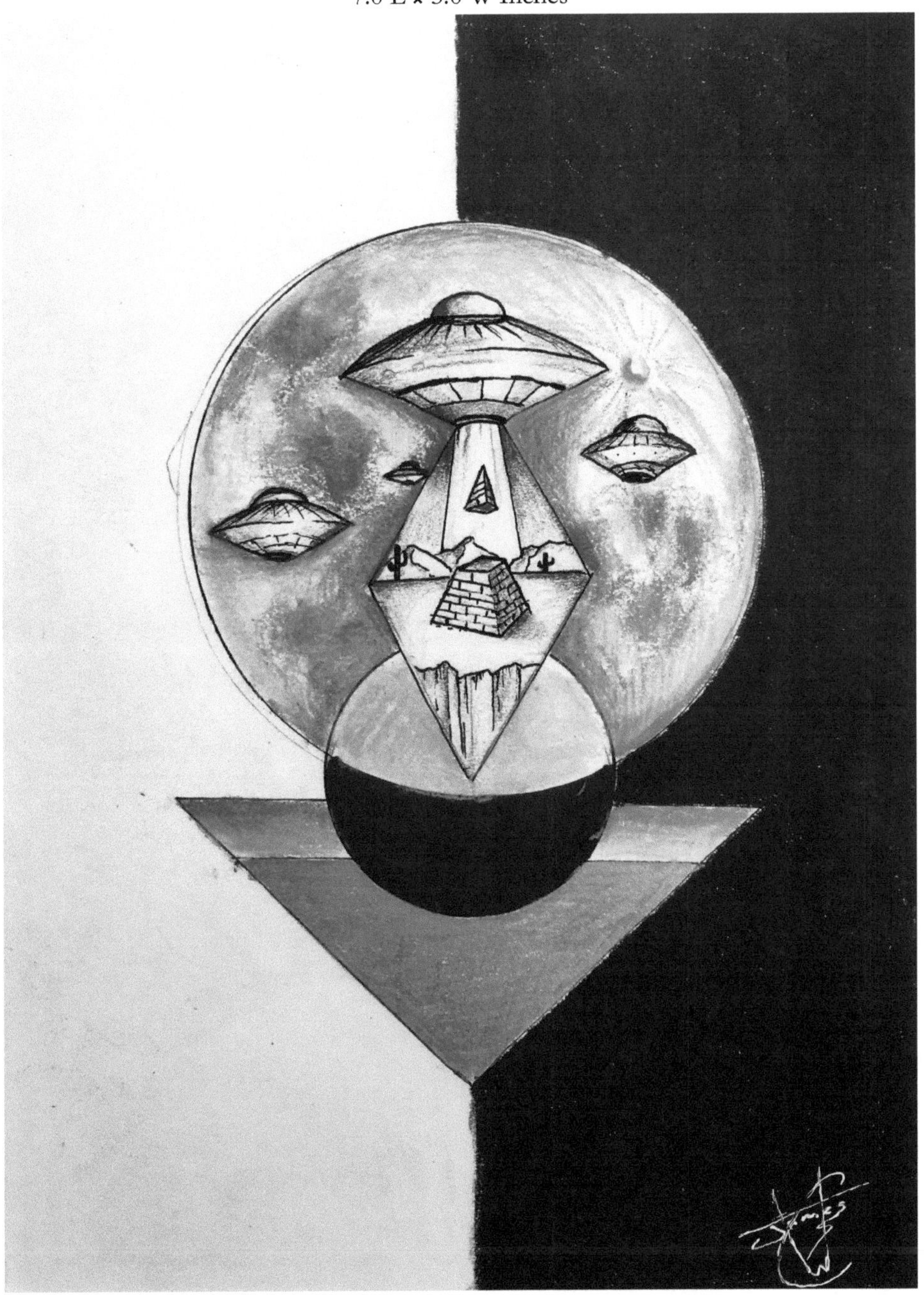

On Display in the Private Art Collection of
Casa de Flamingo's Egyptian Room, Minnesota
Reprinted with Permission

"Helios"
2019

Paper
Colored Pencil
19.0 L × 24.0 W Inches

In the Archives of the James William Christenson Art Gallery, Prior Lake, Minnesota

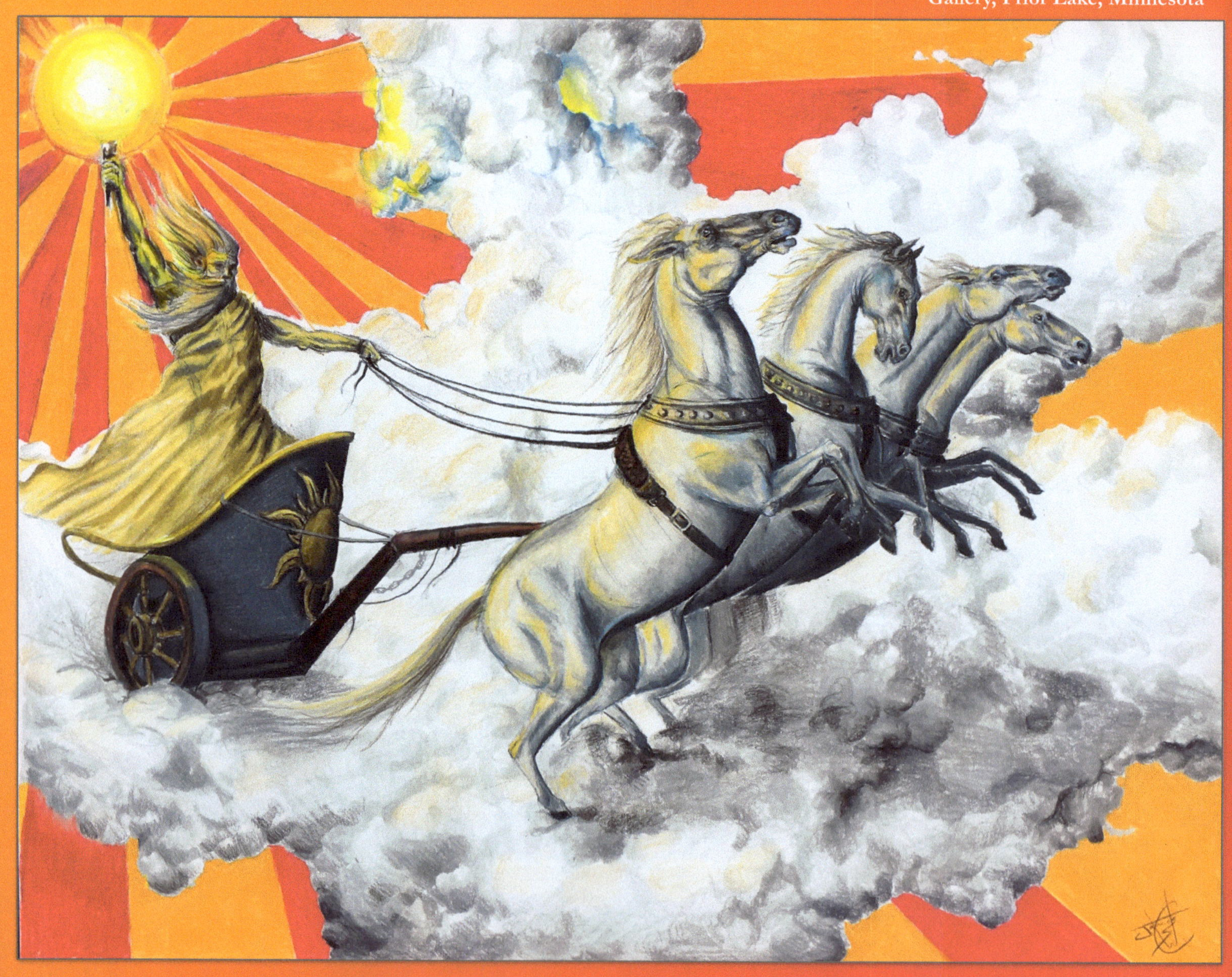

"King of the Tyrant Lizards"
2018

Paper
Pencil Sketch

9.0 L × 12.0 W Inches

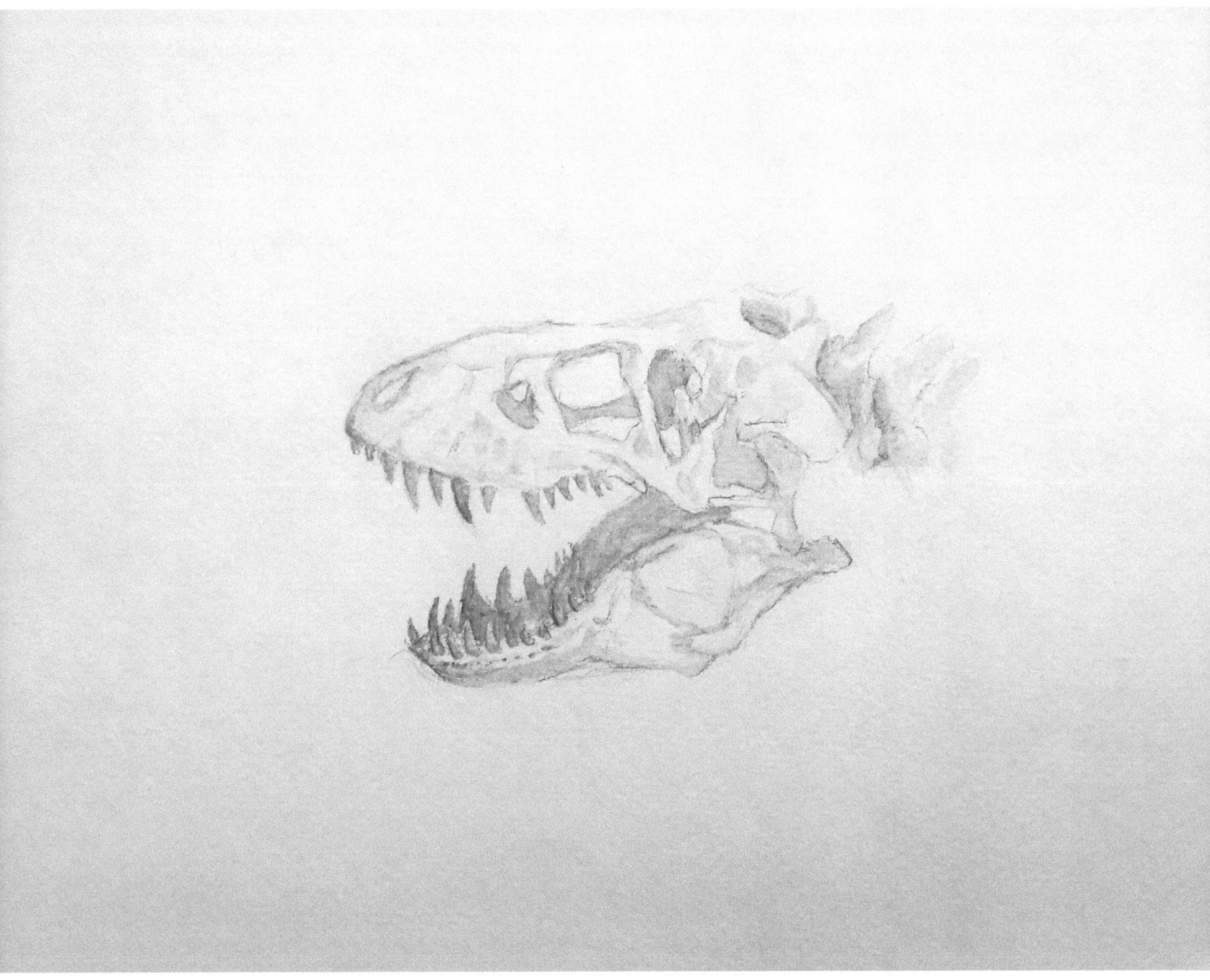

In the Archives of the James William Christenson Art Gallery, Prior Lake, Minnesota

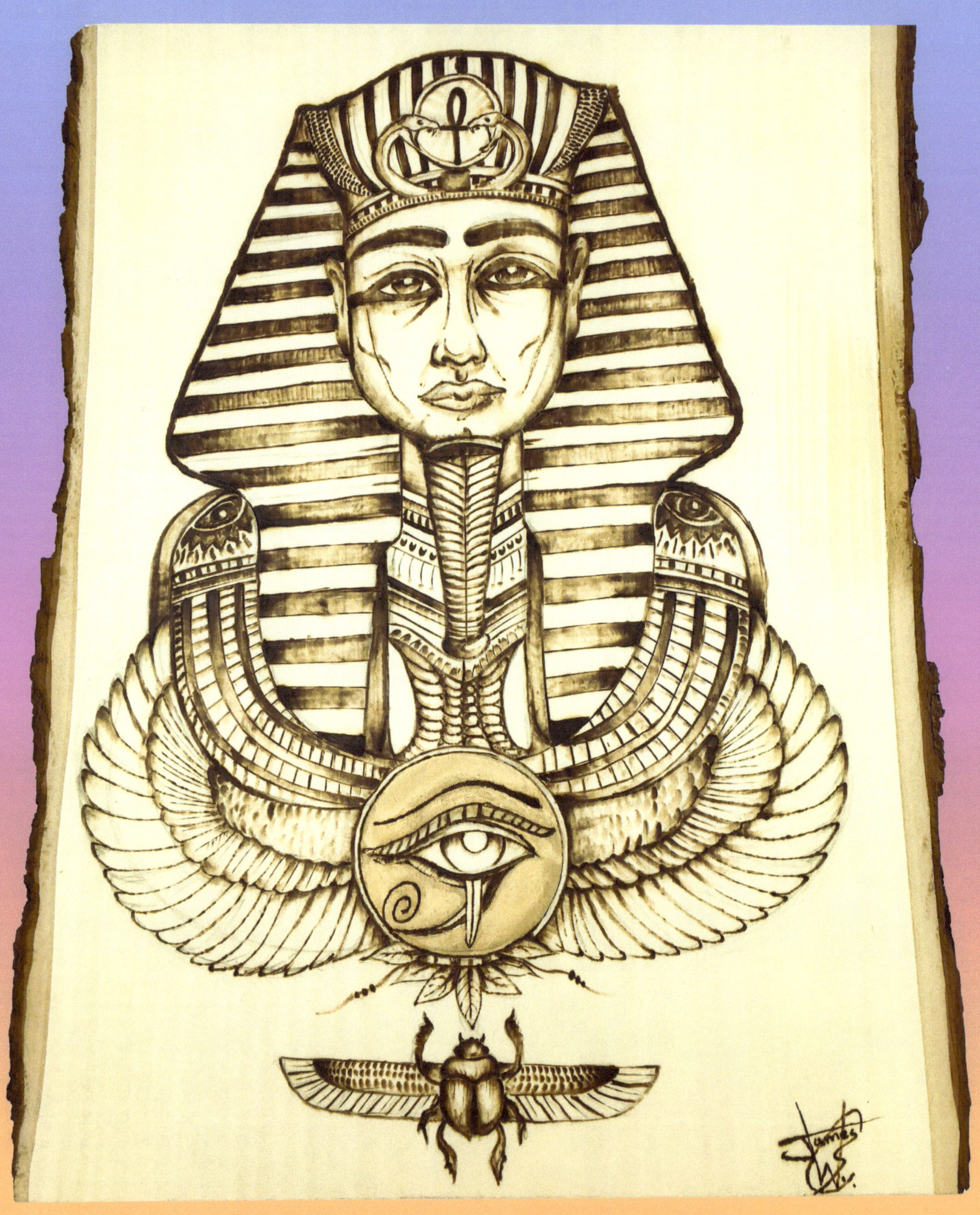

"Pharaoh"
2 Sided
2019

Live Edge, Unfinished Pine Board
Woodburn, Metallic Wax
16.25 L × 12.0 W Inches

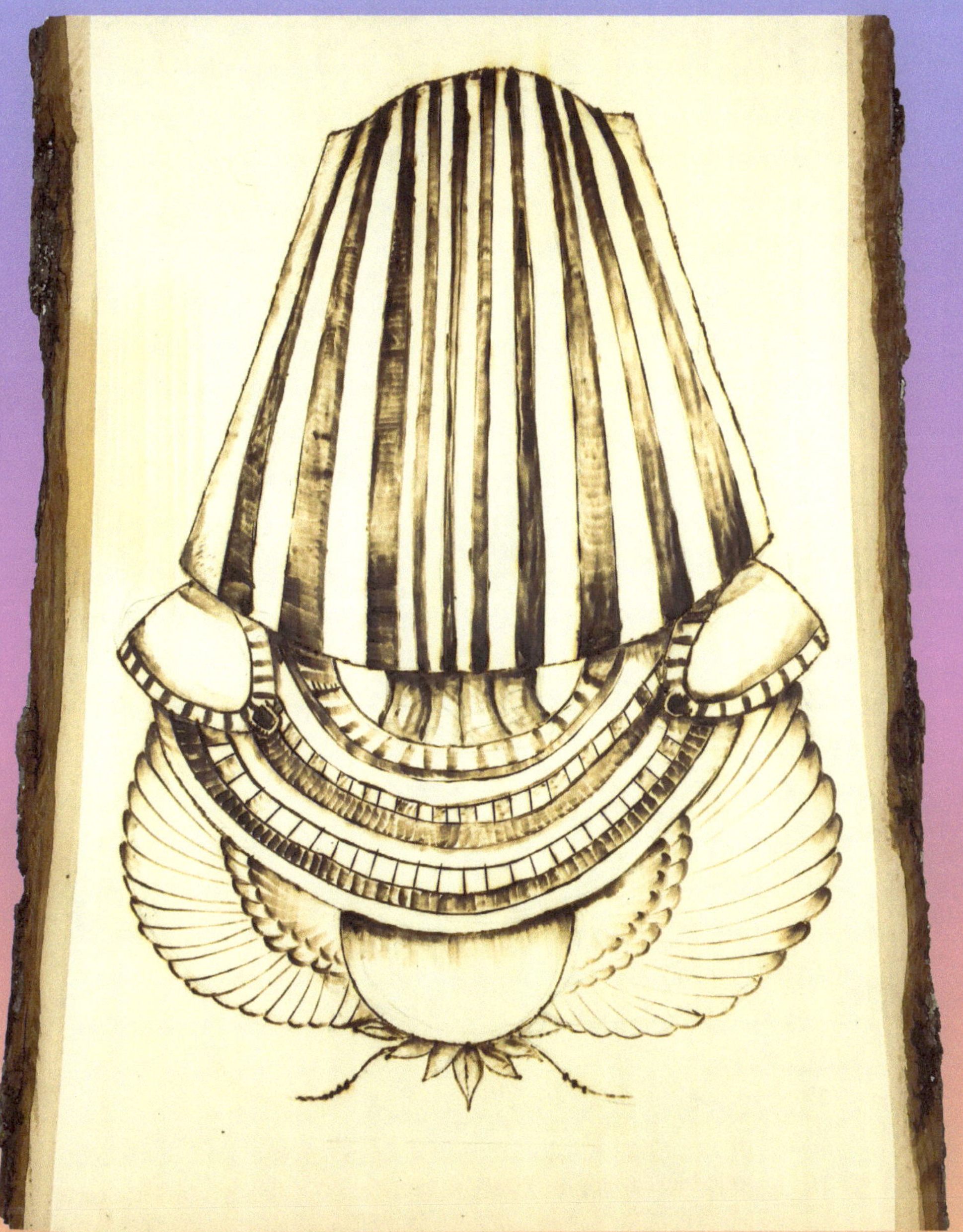

Commissioned for Display in the Private Art Collection of Casa de Flamingo's Egyptian Room, Minnesota
Reprinted with Permission

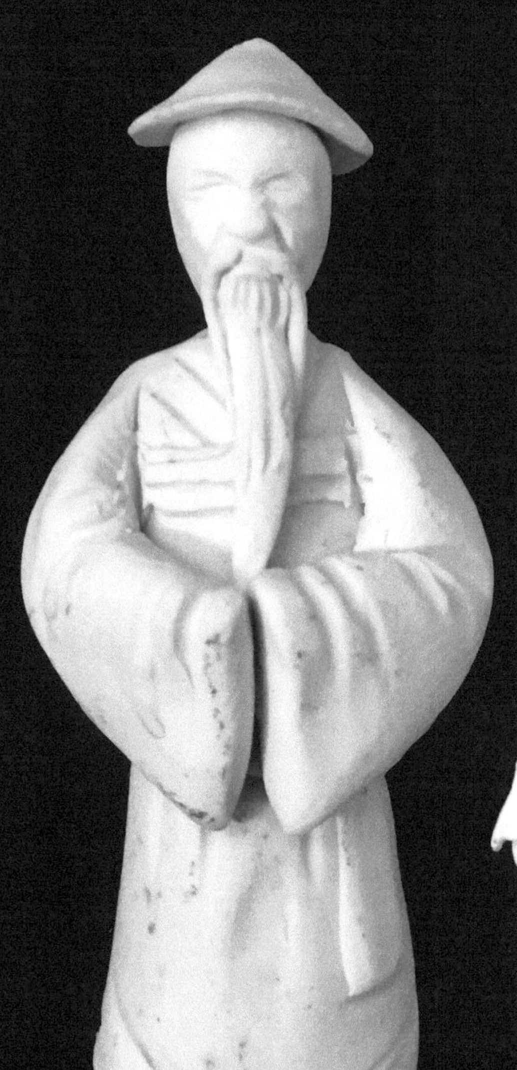

Obverse

"Master of Martial Arts"

Game Piece. Part of a 10 Piece Set.
Made for Custom Designed Onitama® Board Game.
2017

Polymer Clay

1.75 H × 0.75 W Inches

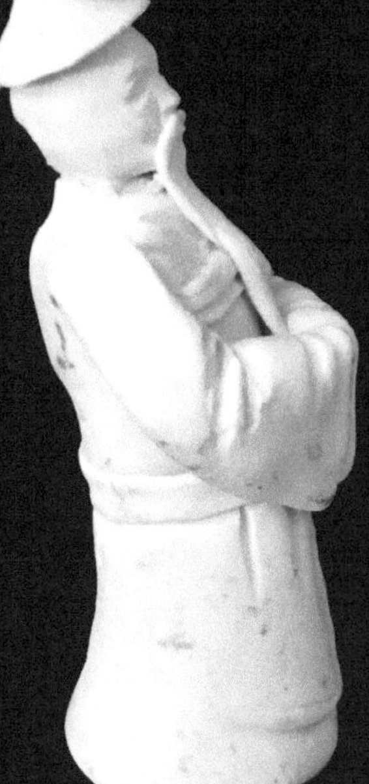

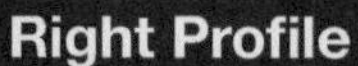

Right Profile

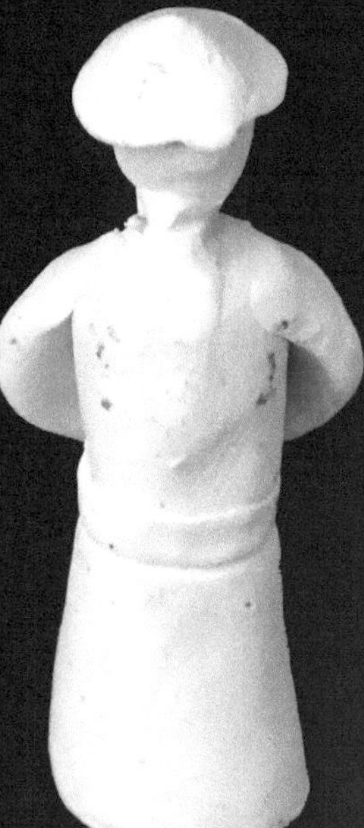

Reverse

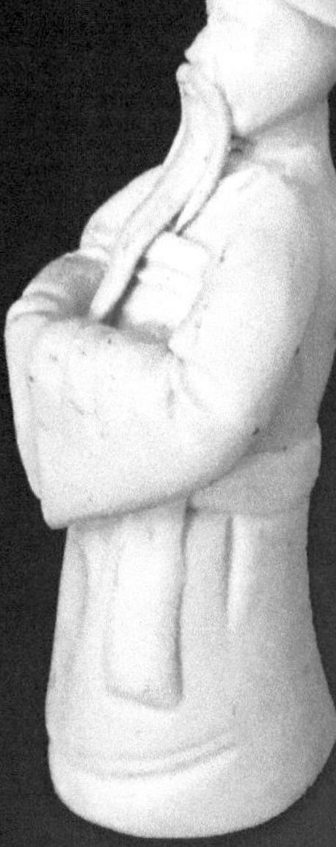

Left Profile

Presented as a Gift. Custom Designed & Created Onitama® Game for Use & Display in the Private Art Collection of Casa de Flamingo, Minnesota
Reprinted with Permission

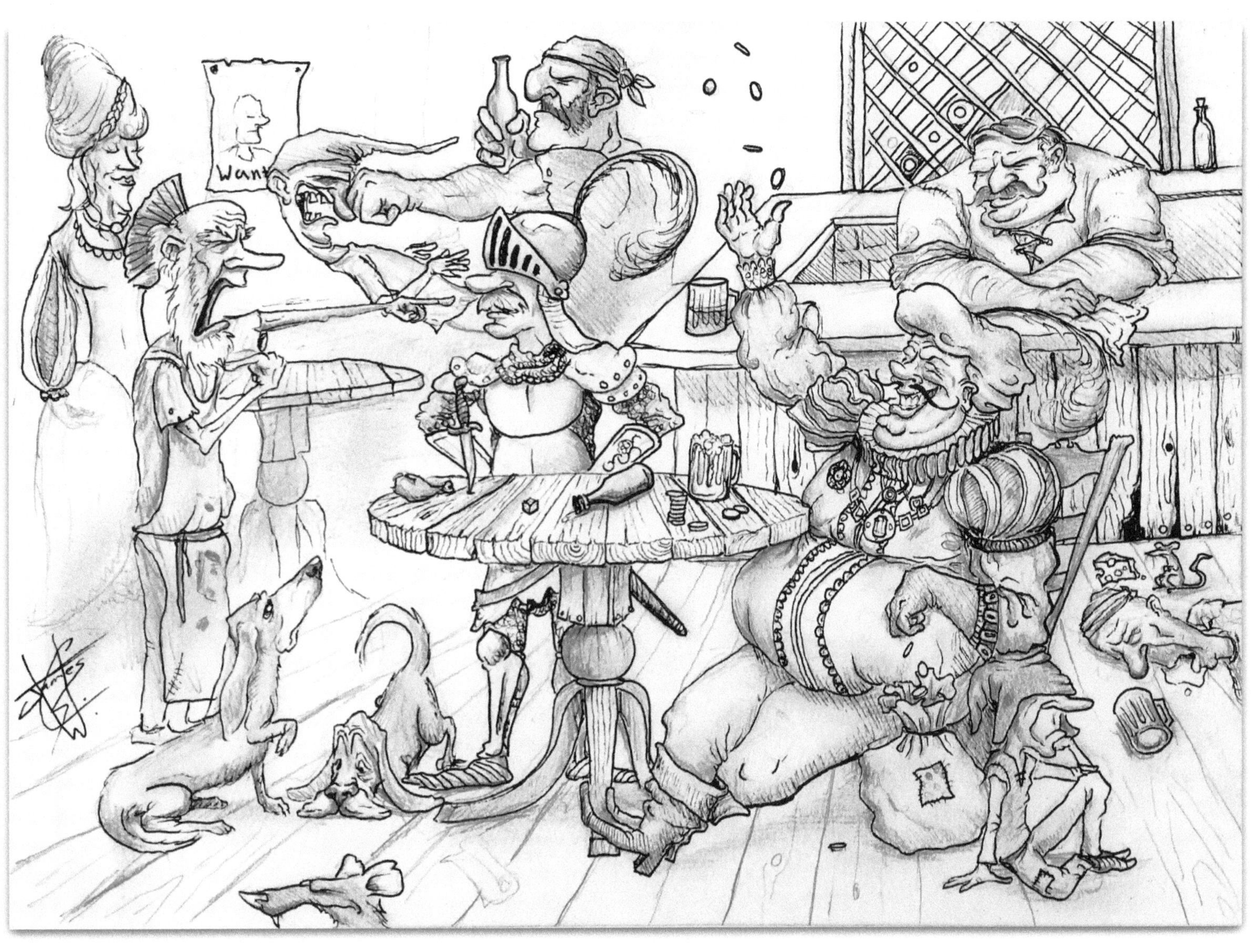

"Sheriff of Nottingham"
2019

Paper
Pencil & Pen Sketch
8.5 L × 11.0 W Inches

In the Archives of the
James William Christenson Art Gallery
Prior Lake, Minnesota

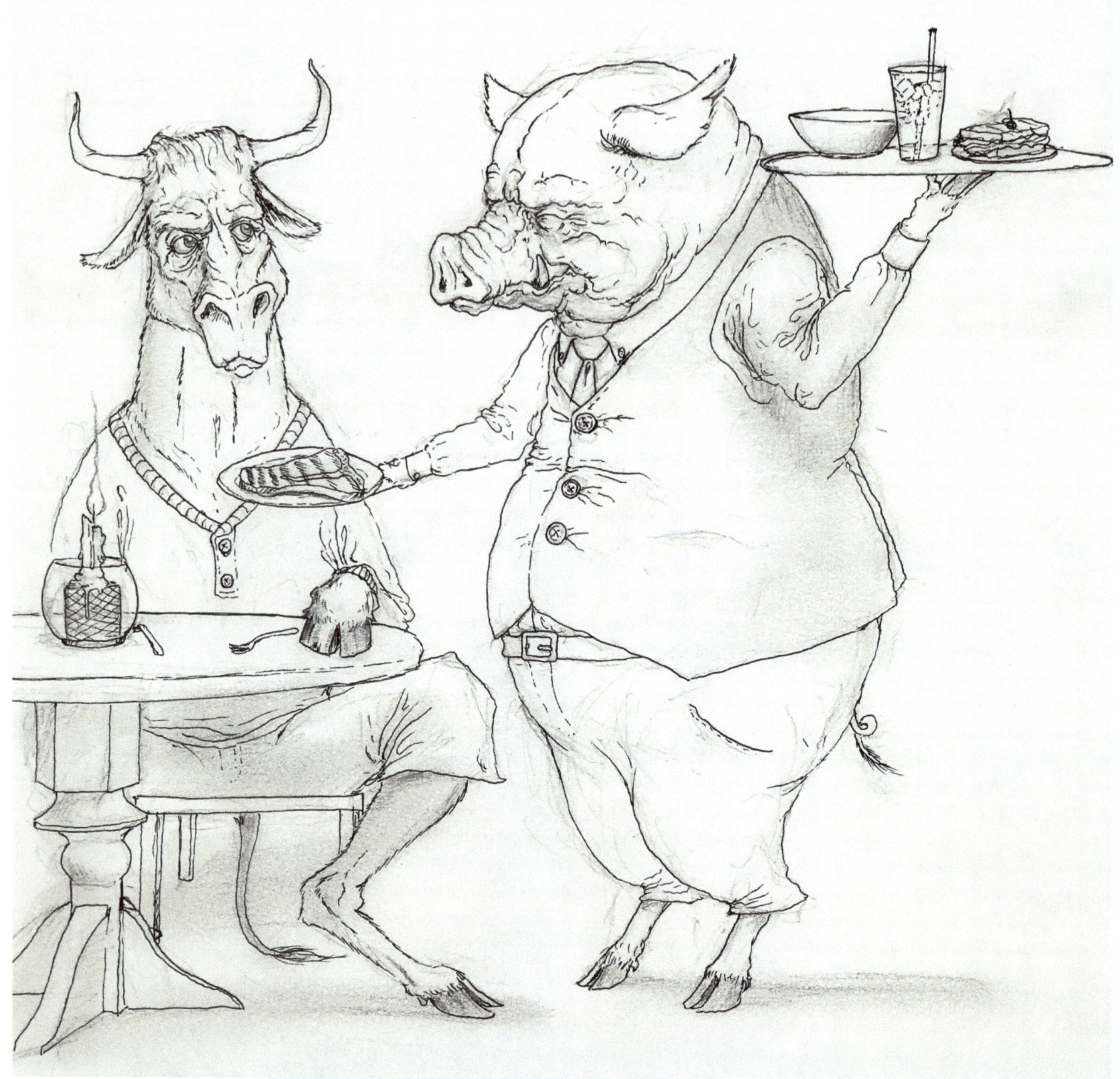

"I Ordered Bacon"
2018

Paper
Pencil & Pen Sketch
8.5 L × 11.0 W Inches

In the Archives of the James William Christenson Art Gallery, Prior Lake, Minnesota

"Axis Powers"
From the **WWII Caricature** Series
2017

Polymer Clay
2.0 L × 1.3 W Inches

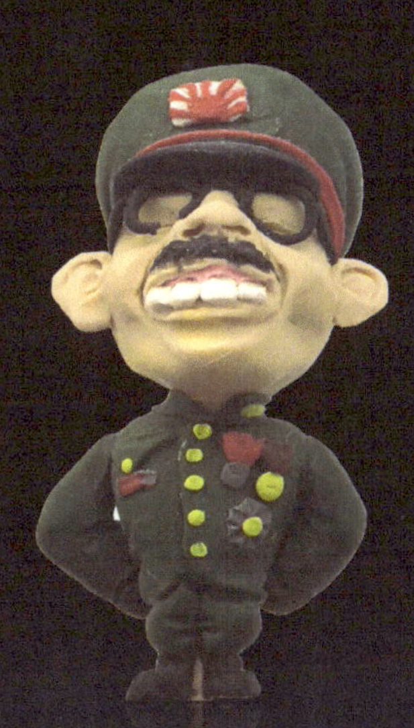

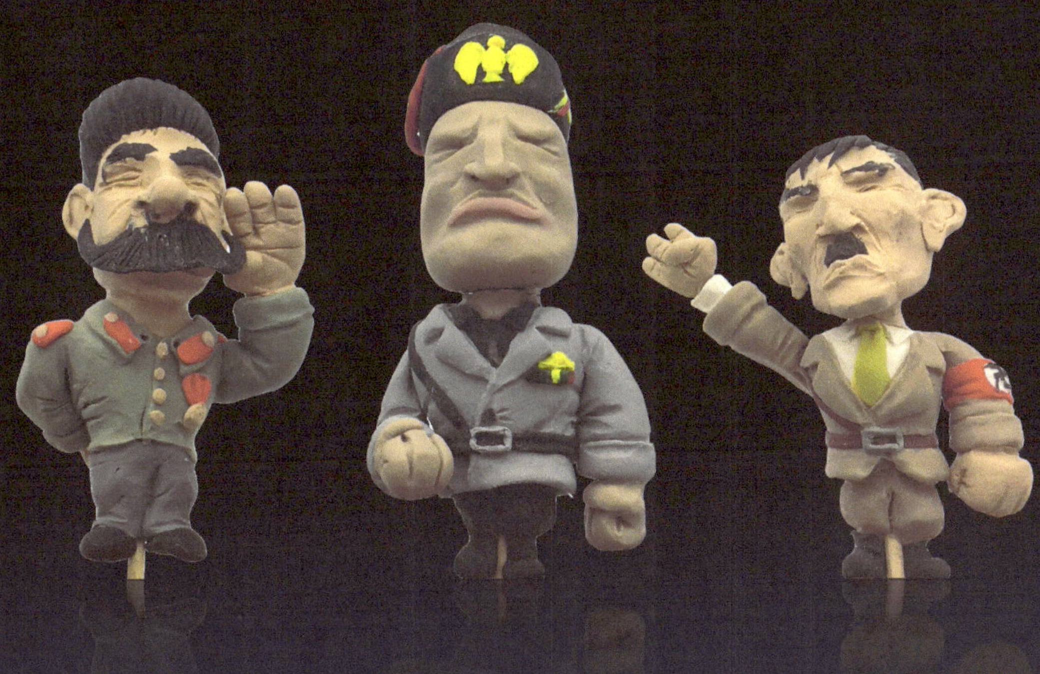

In the Archives of the James
William Christenson Art Gallery
Prior Lake, Minnesota

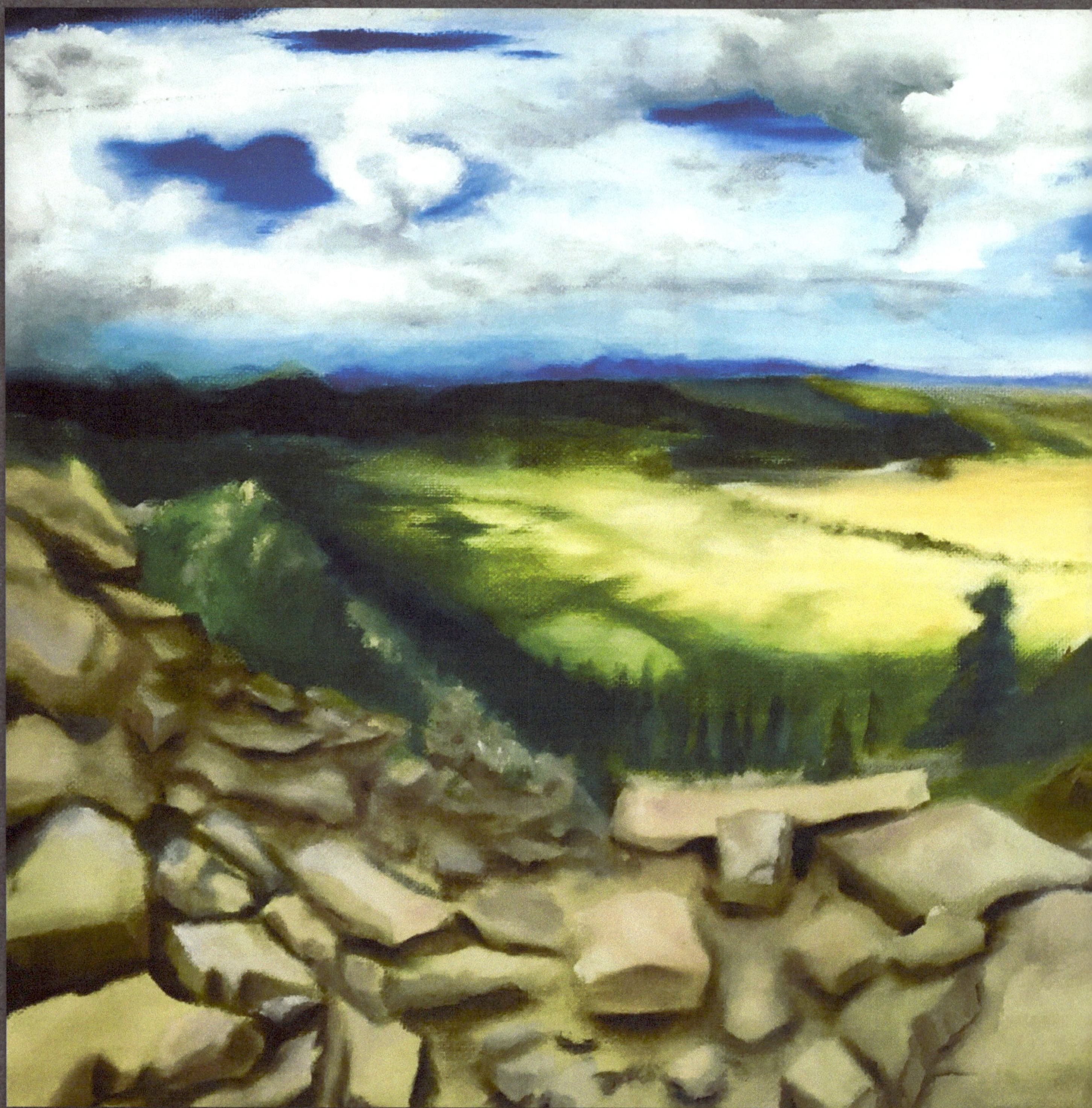

"Three Mountain Top Experiences"

Philmont Ranch, Rocky Mountain High Desert
New Mexico, USA
2016

Stretched Canvas Over Wooden Frame

Oil
24.0 L × 12.0 W Inches

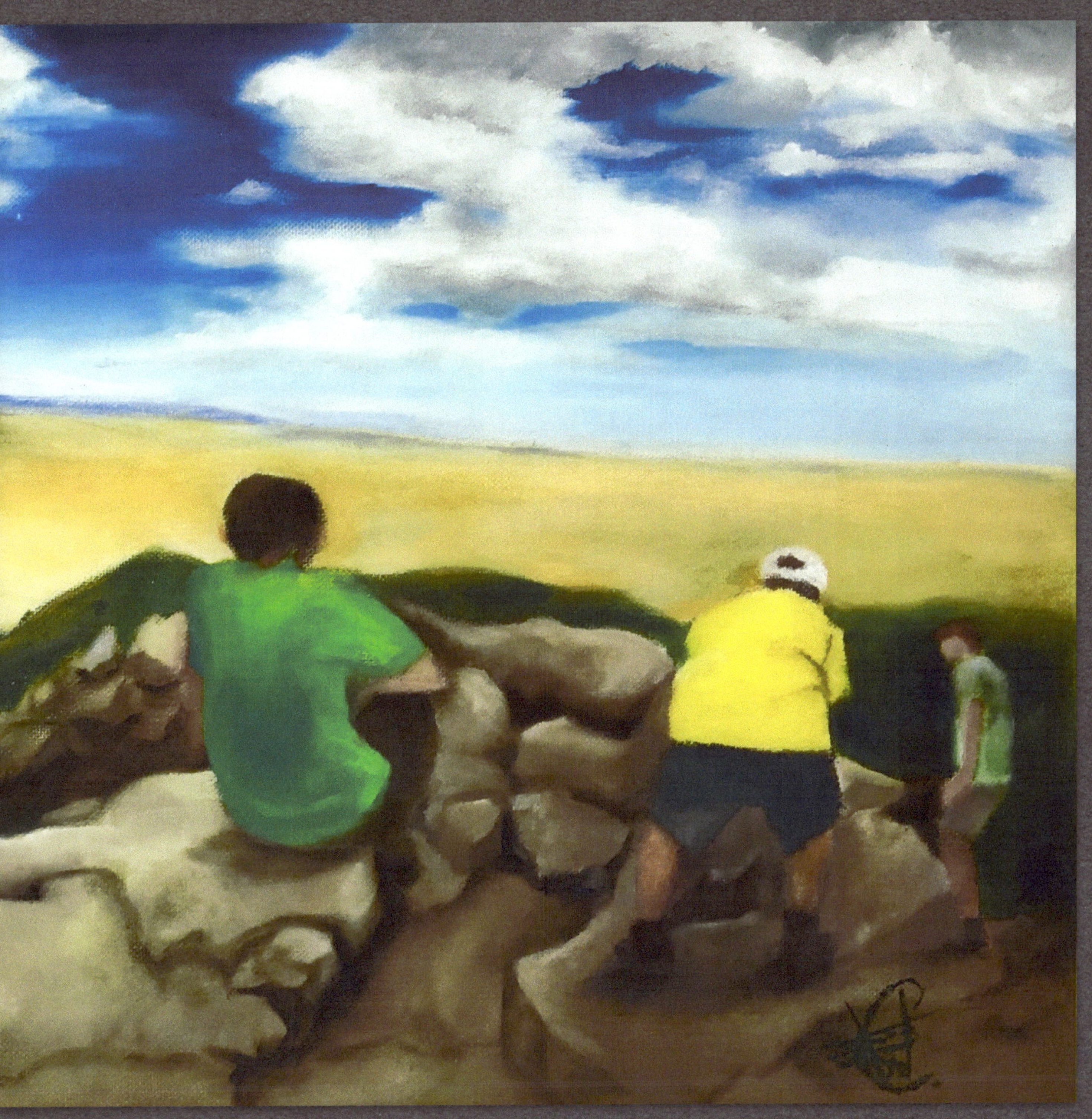

Presented as a Gift.
On Display in the Private Art Collection of
Casa de Flamingo, Minnesota
Reprinted with Permission

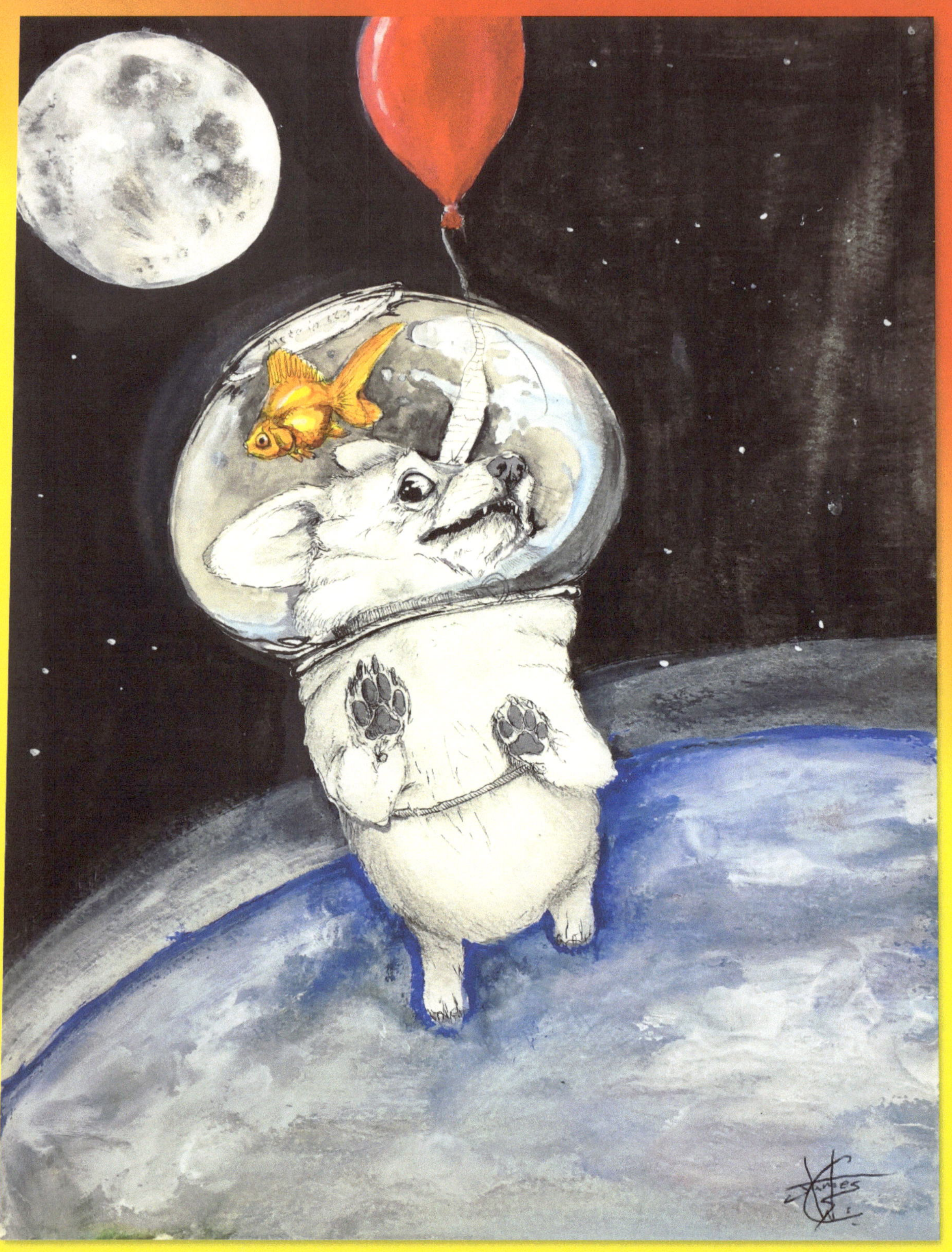

"Pisces & Sirius"
2016

Paper
Acrylic, Pen, Pencil
12.0 L × 9.0 W Inches

In the Archives of the James William Christenson Art Gallery Prior Lake, Minnesota

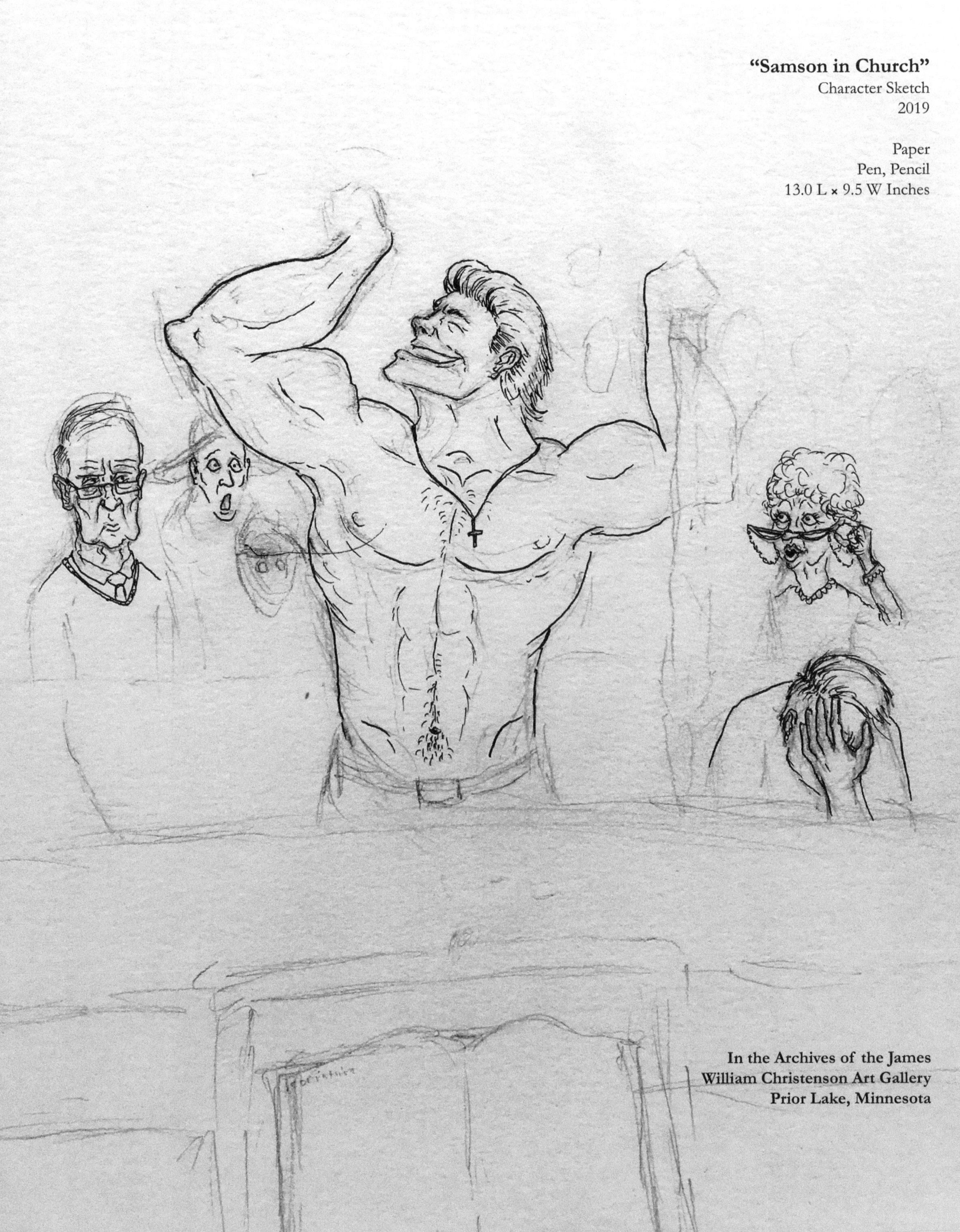

"Samson in Church"
Character Sketch
2019

Paper
Pen, Pencil
13.0 L × 9.5 W Inches

In the Archives of the James William Christenson Art Gallery Prior Lake, Minnesota

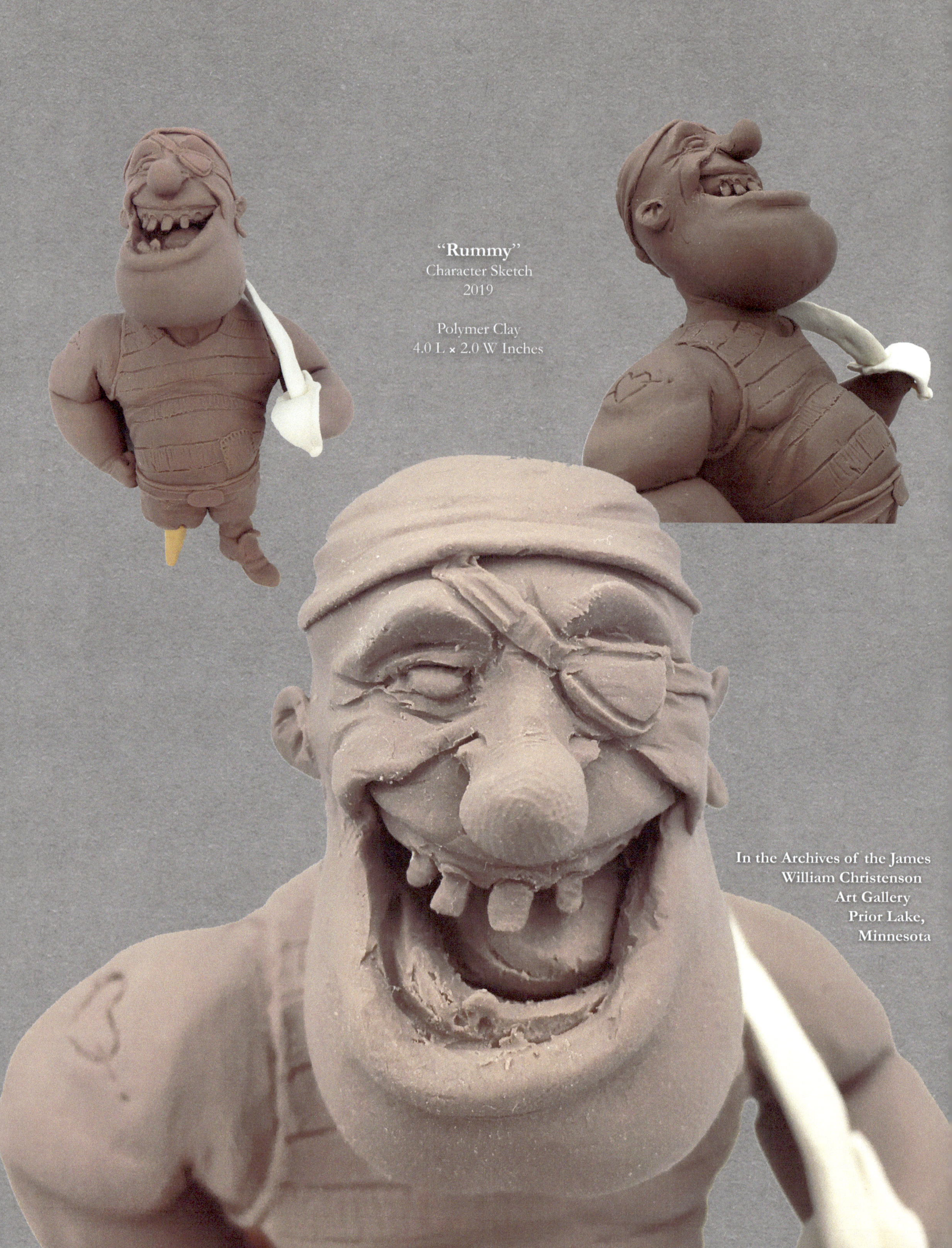

"**Rummy**"
Character Sketch
2019

Polymer Clay
4.0 L × 2.0 W Inches

In the Archives of the James William Christenson Art Gallery Prior Lake, Minnesota

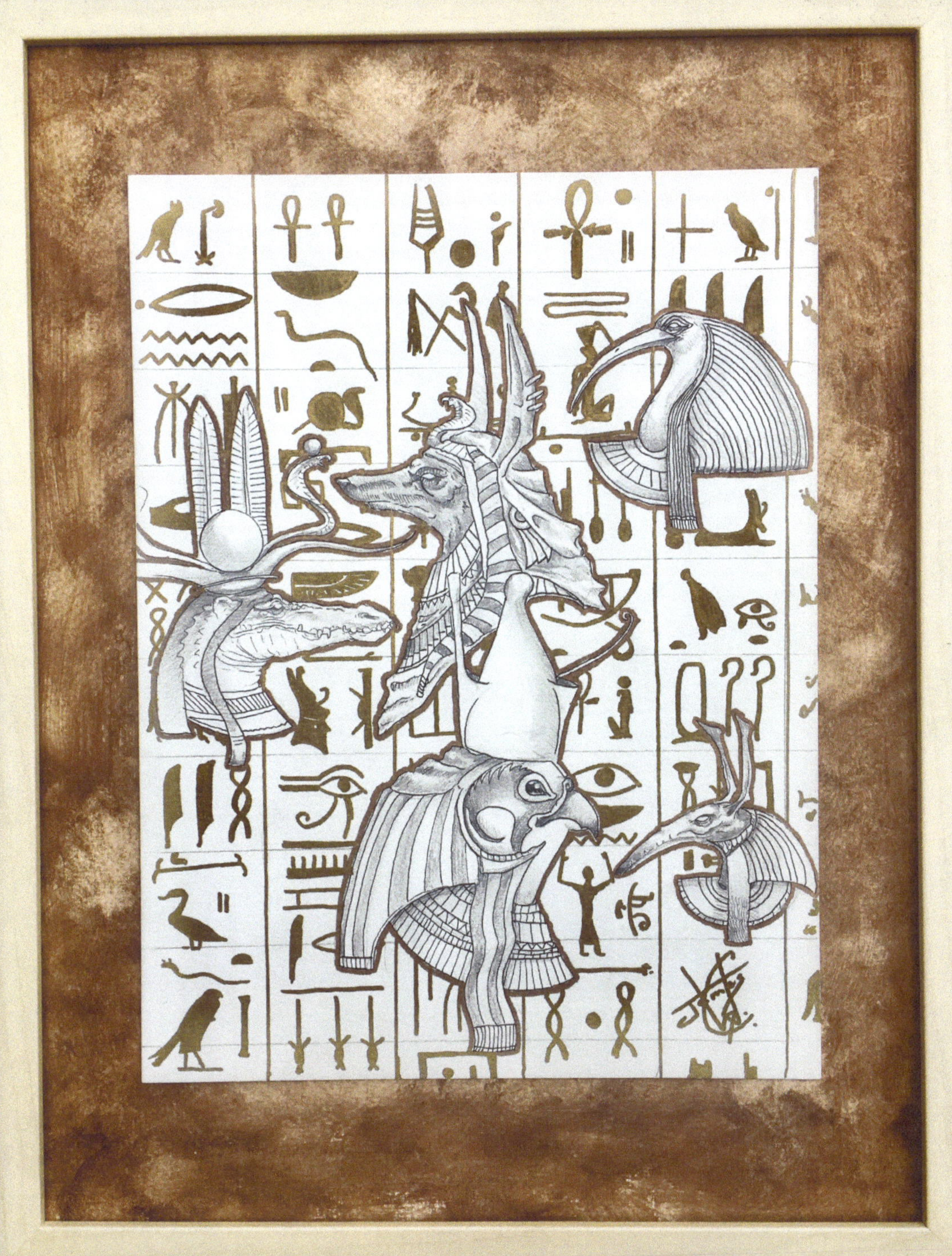

Commissioned for Display in the Private Art Collection of Casa de Flamingo's Egyptian Room, Minnesota
Reprinted with Permission

"Egyptian Gods"
2019

Paper, Mat, Unfinished Maple Frame
Pen, Pencil, Felt Marker, Watercolor
16.8 L × 12.8 W Inches

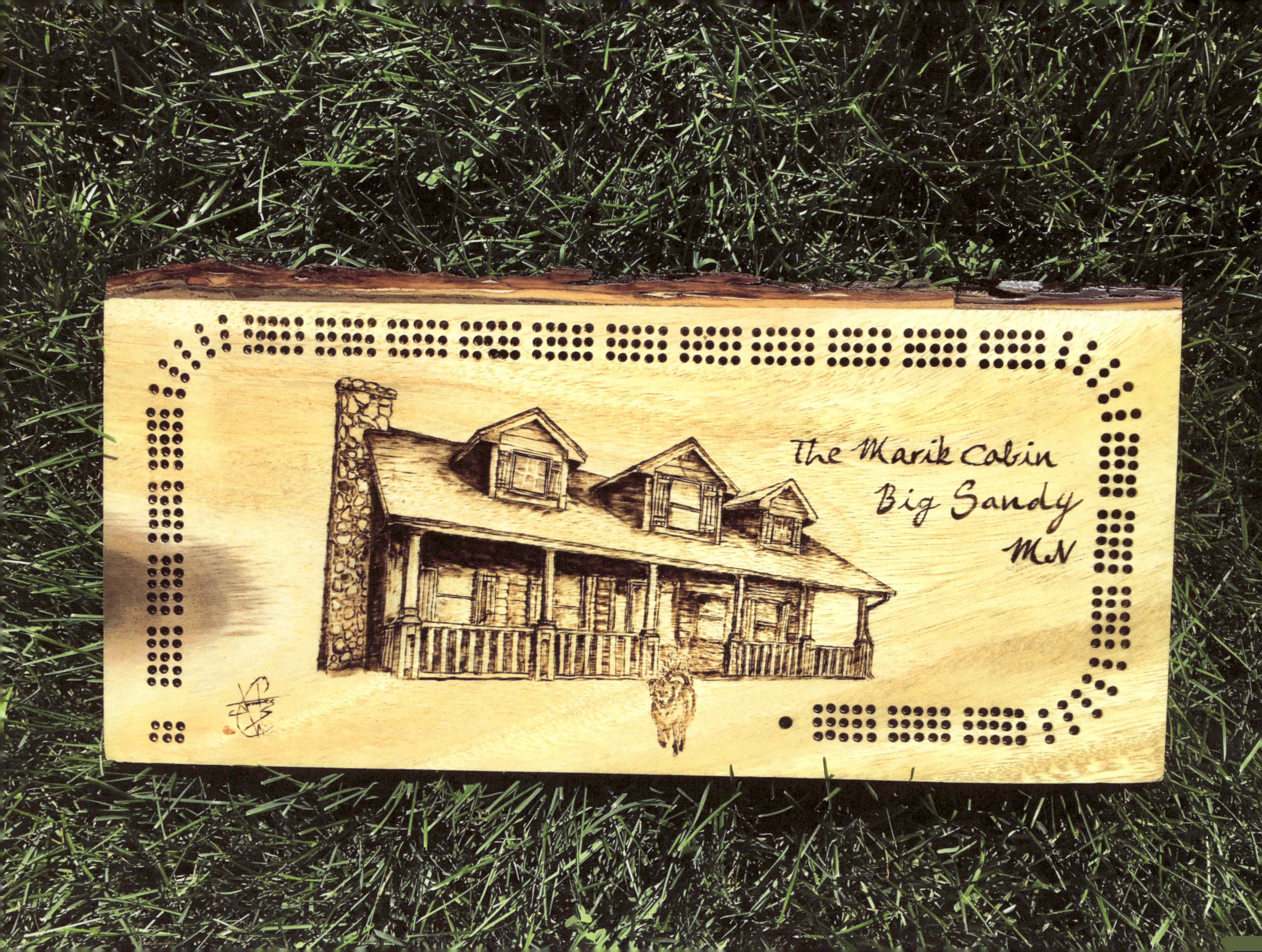
The Marik Cabin
Big Sandy
MN

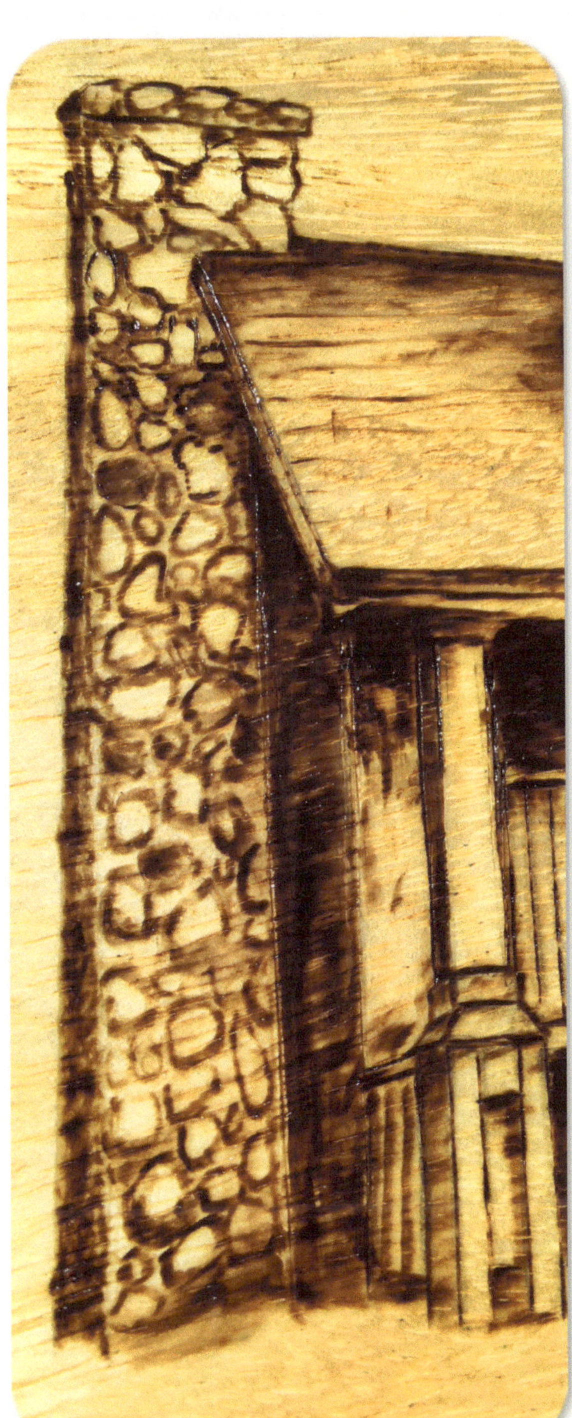

Chimney Detail

“Cabin Cribbage Board”
2019

Live Edge, Finished Acacia Wood Board
Woodburn, Lacquer
17.25 L × 8.5 W Inches

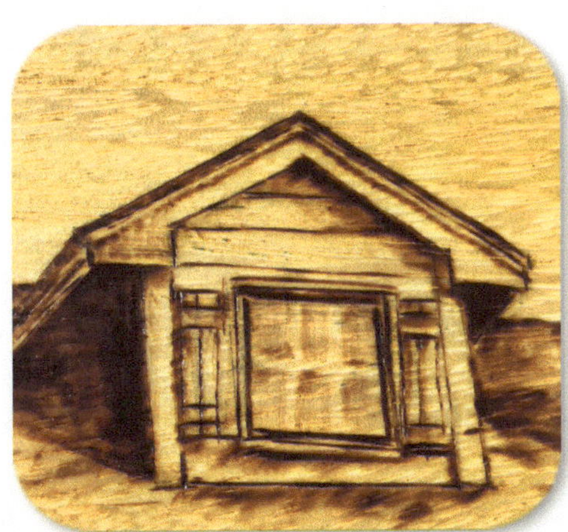

Window Detail

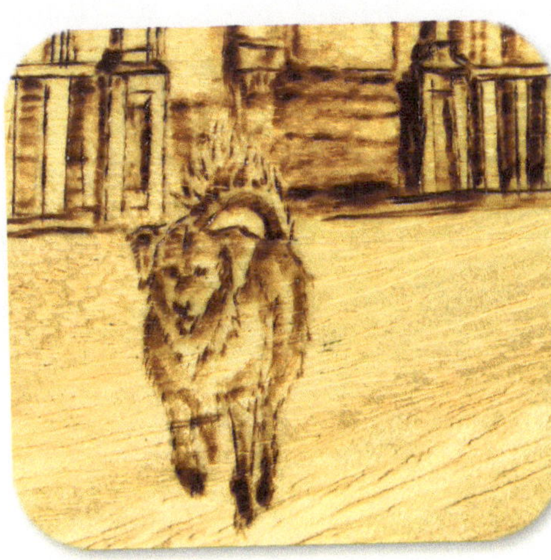

Dog Detail

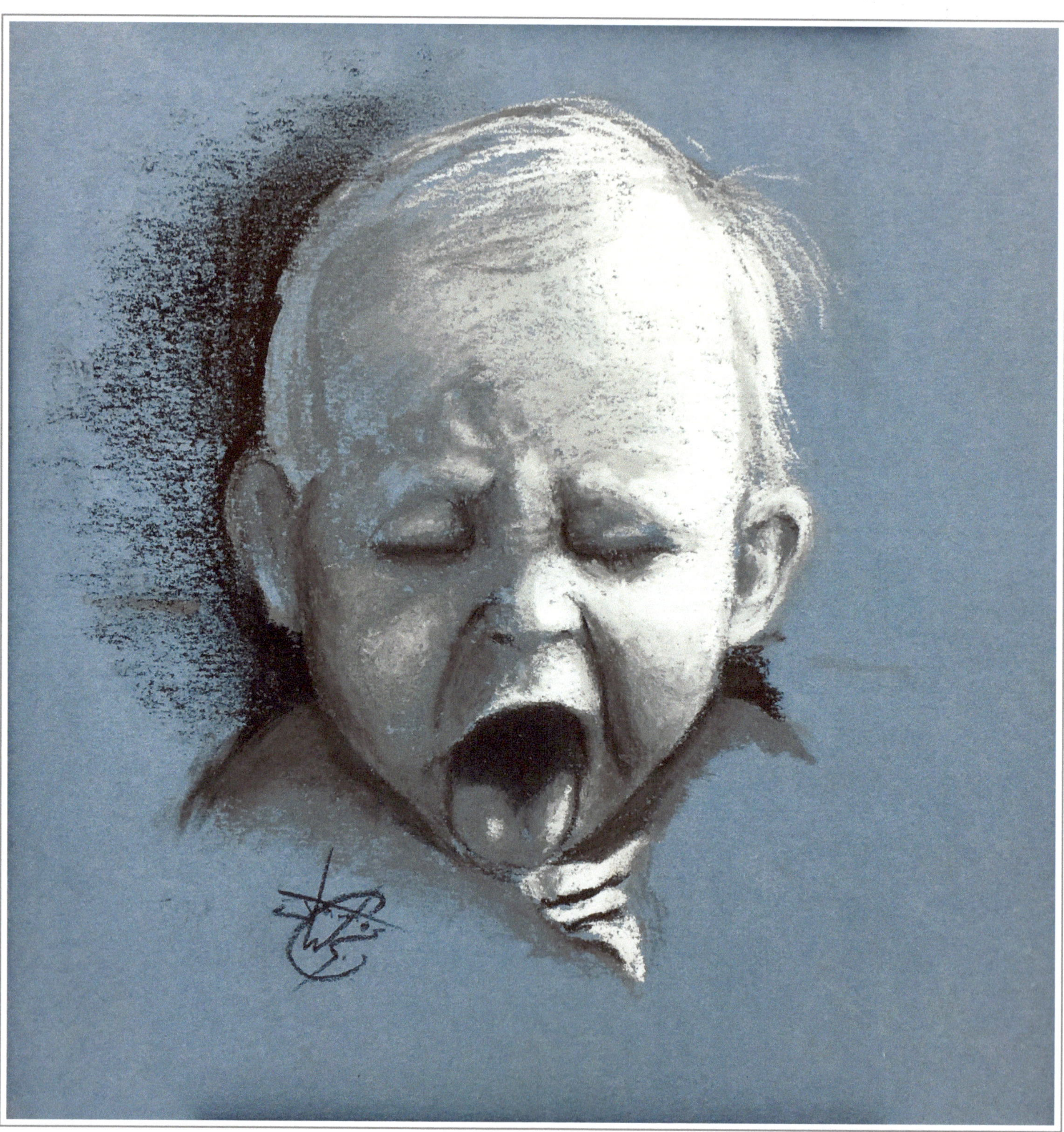

"Eleanor"
2019

Paper
Pastel
8.0 L × 8.0 W Inches

In the Archives of the James William Christenson Art Gallery Prior Lake, Minnesota

In the Archives of the James
William Christenson Art Gallery
Prior Lake, Minnesota

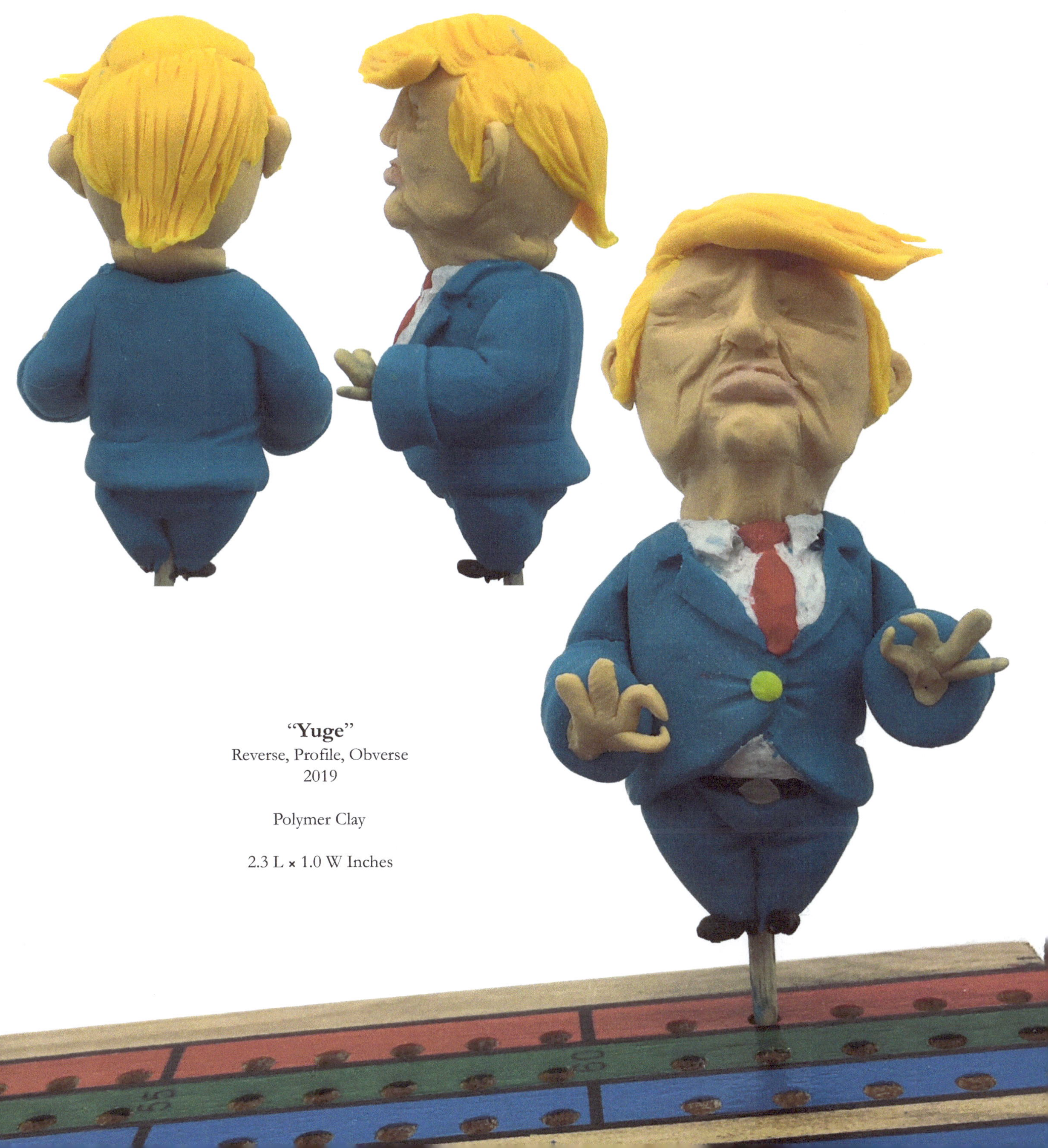

"Yuge"
Reverse, Profile, Obverse
2019

Polymer Clay

2.3 L × 1.0 W Inches

"Waiting"
After John Singer Sargent: Muddy Alligators
2018

Paper
Watercolor
12.0 L × 16.5 W Inches

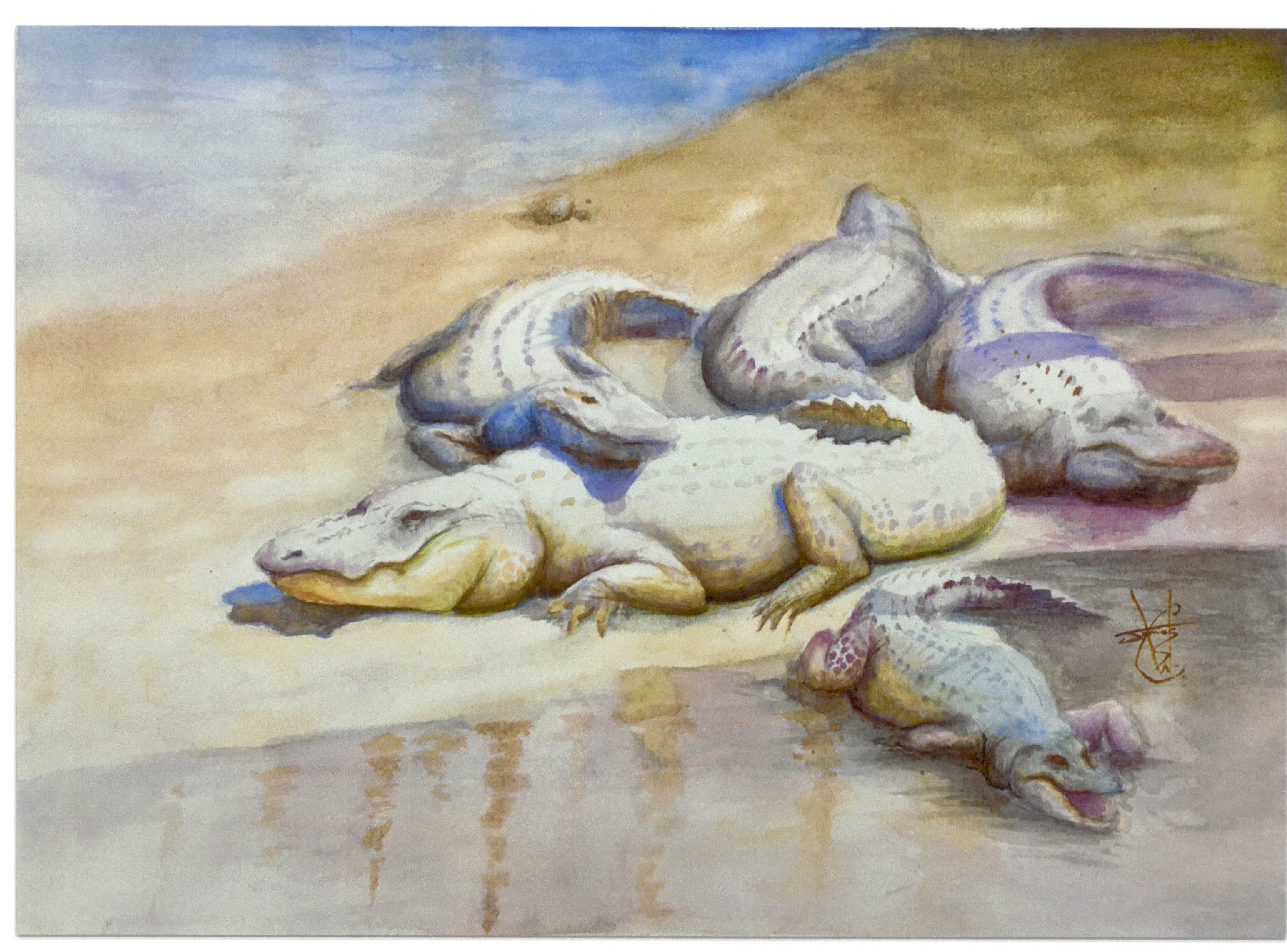

In the Archives of the James William Christenson Art Gallery Prior Lake, Minnesota

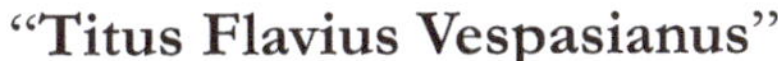

"Titus Flavius Vespasianus"
Character Doodle
2018

Polymer Clay
1.0 L × 1.0 W Inches

In the Archives of the James William Christenson Art Gallery Prior Lake, Minnesota

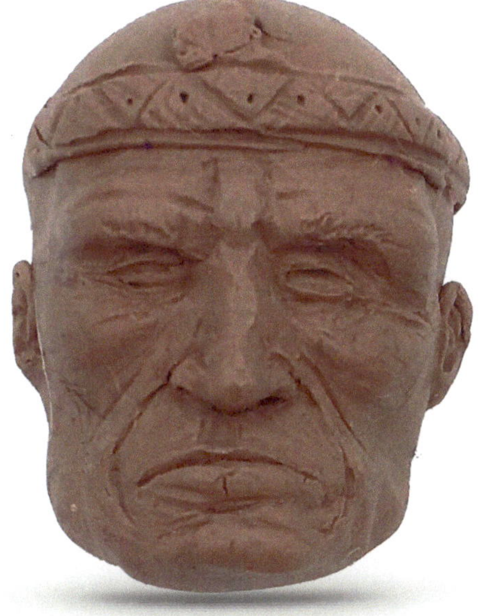

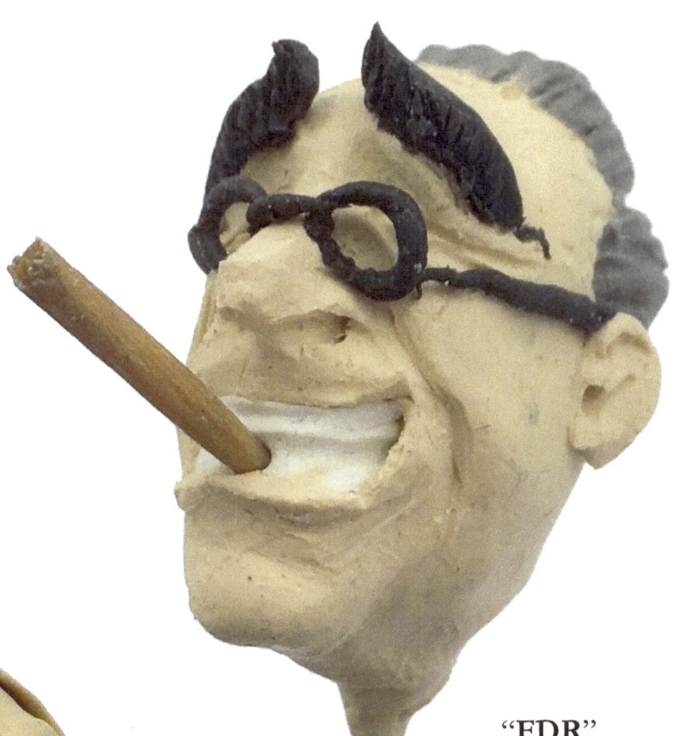

"FDR"
Character Sketch
2018

Polymer Clay, Toothpick
1.5 L × 1.0 W Inches

"Laughing Imp"
2018

Polymer Clay
1.0 L × 1.5 W Inches

"Jesus Calms the Seas"
Wall Mural, Bethesda Church
2018

Latex Wall Paint
8.5 L × 9.0 W Feet

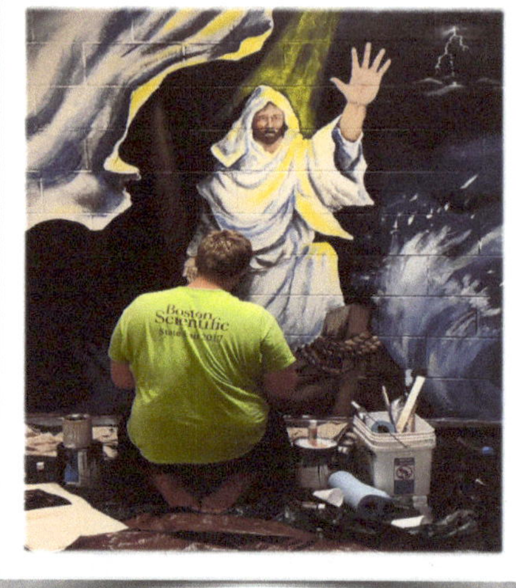

Children's Wing Mural
Bethesda Church
Prior Lake, Minnesota
Reprinted with Permission

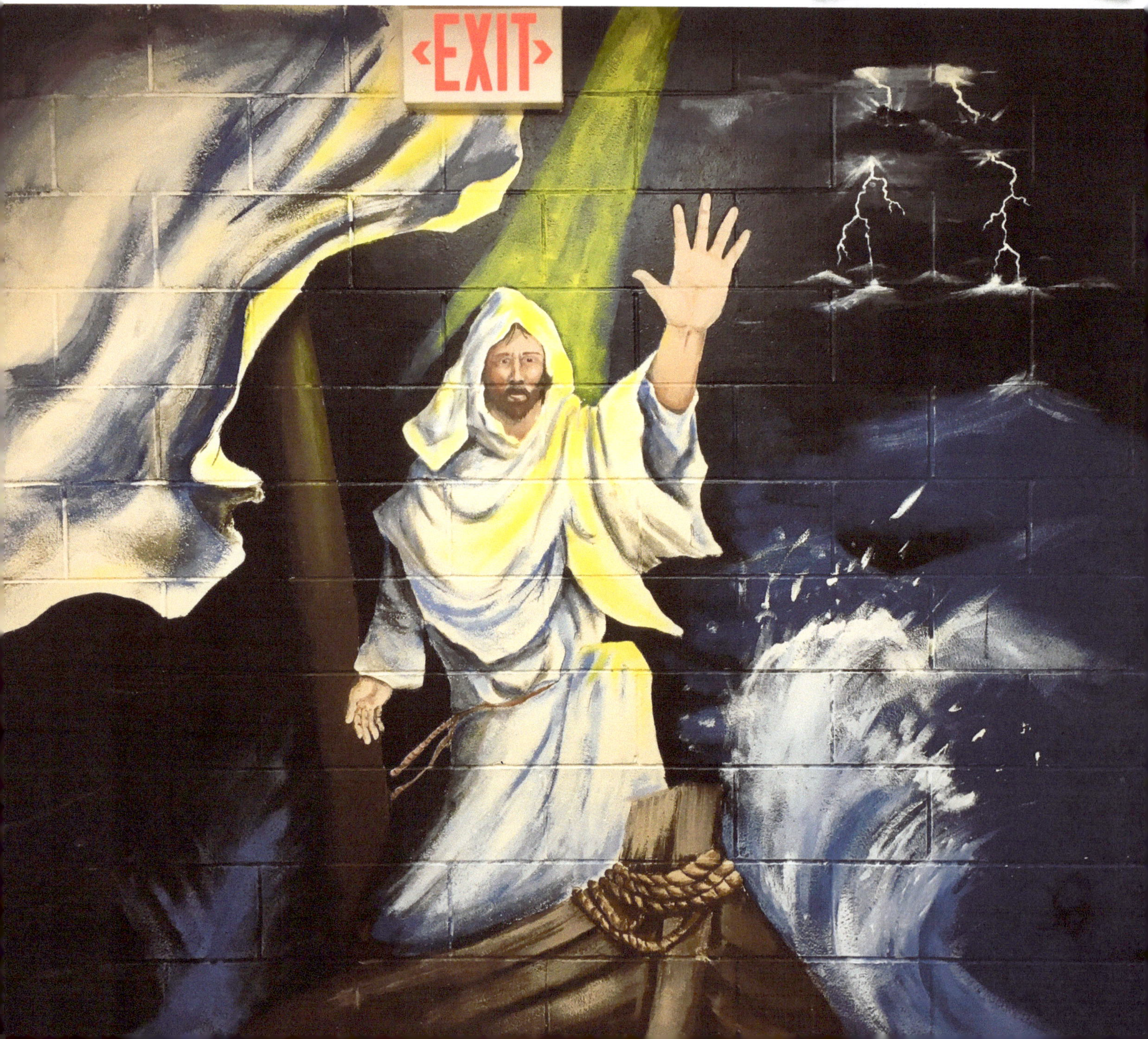

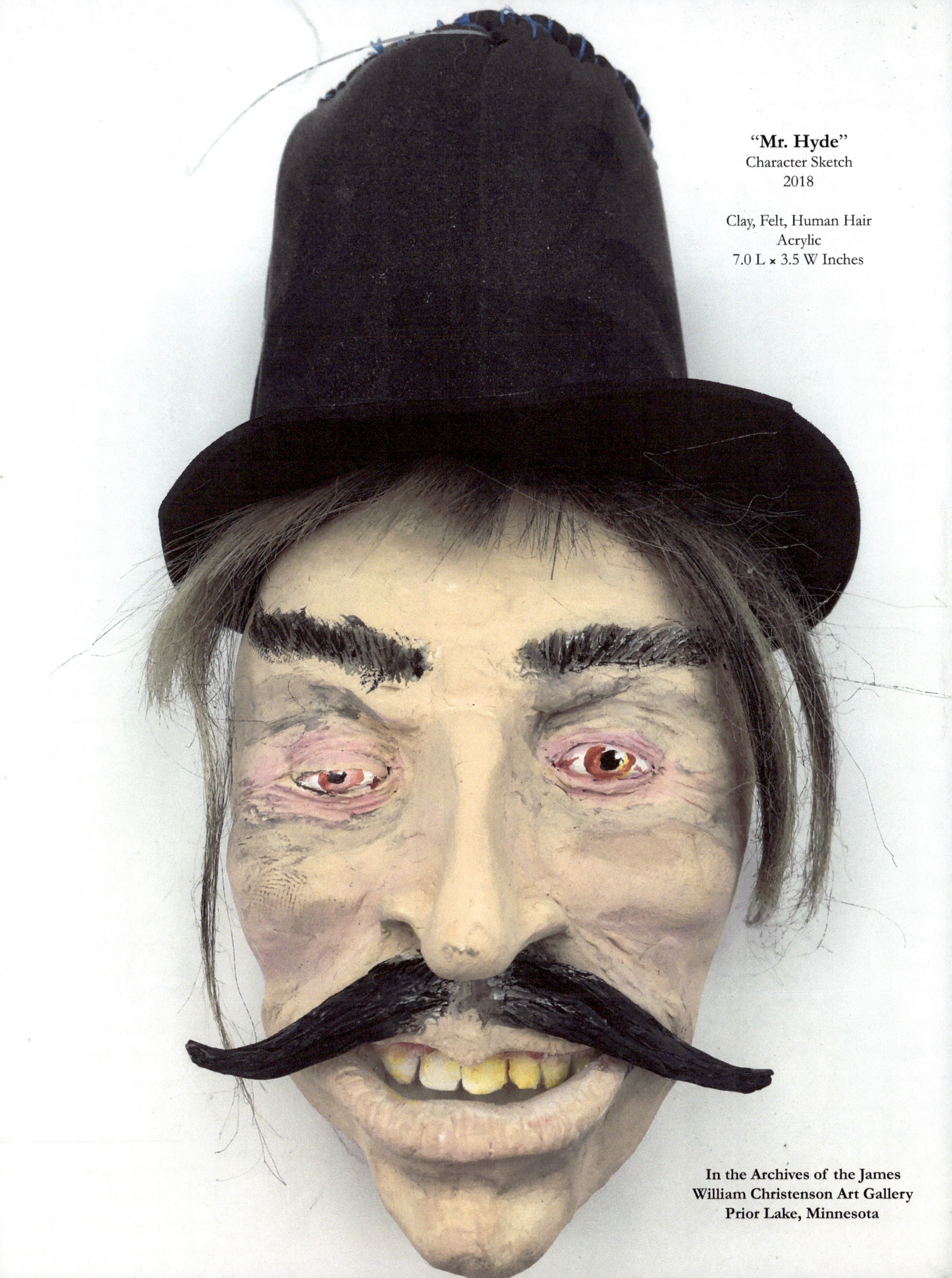

"Mr. Hyde"
Character Sketch
2018

Clay, Felt, Human Hair
Acrylic
7.0 L × 3.5 W Inches

In the Archives of the James William Christenson Art Gallery Prior Lake, Minnesota

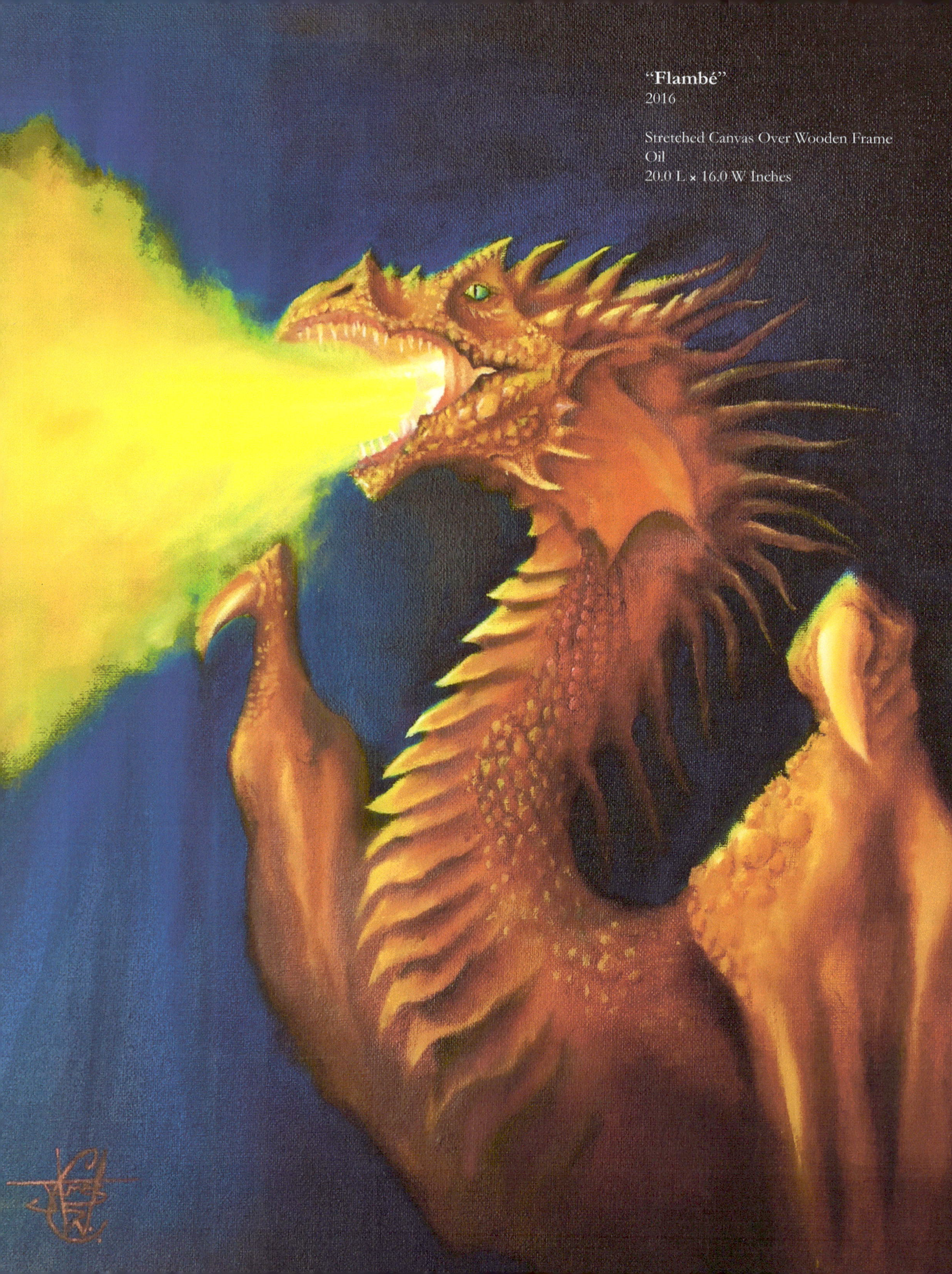

"Flambé"
2016

Stretched Canvas Over Wooden Frame
Oil
20.0 L × 16.0 W Inches

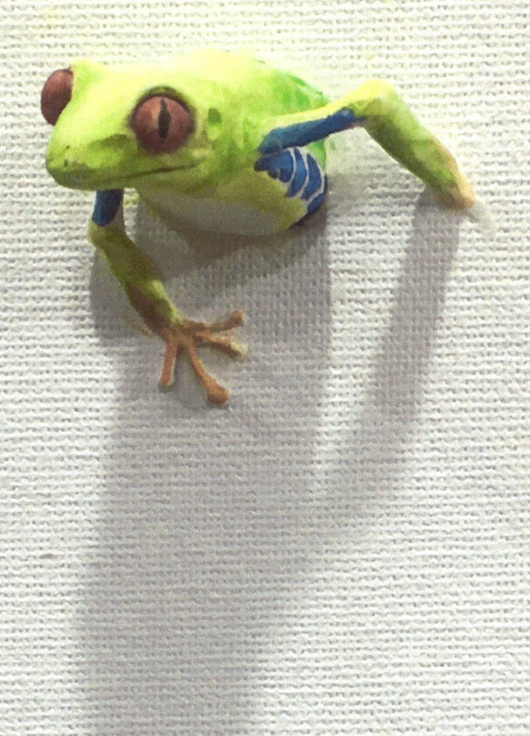

"Emergence"
2017

Canvas Board, Polymer Clay
Acrylic

10.0 L × 8.0 W Inches

In the Archives of the James William Christenson Art Gallery Prior Lake, Minnesota

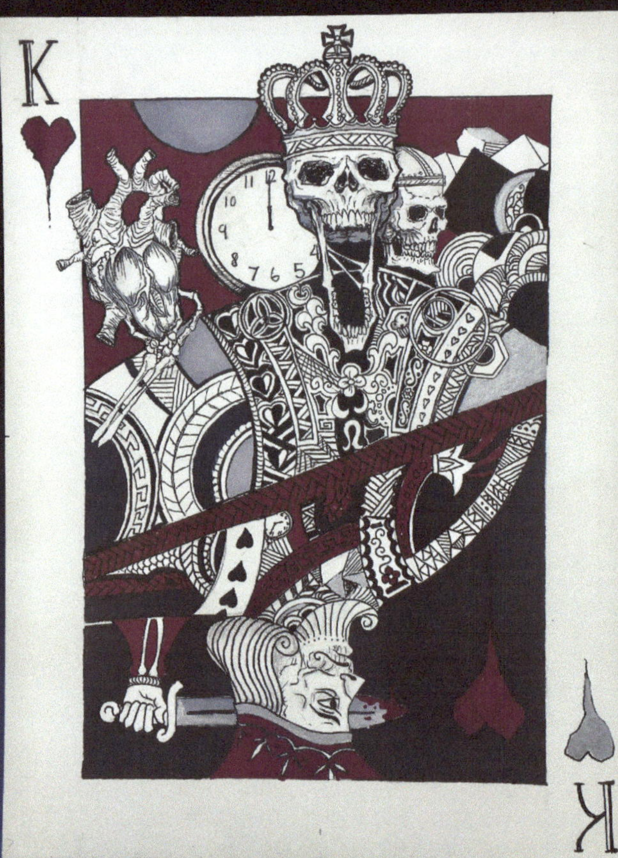

"King of Hearts"

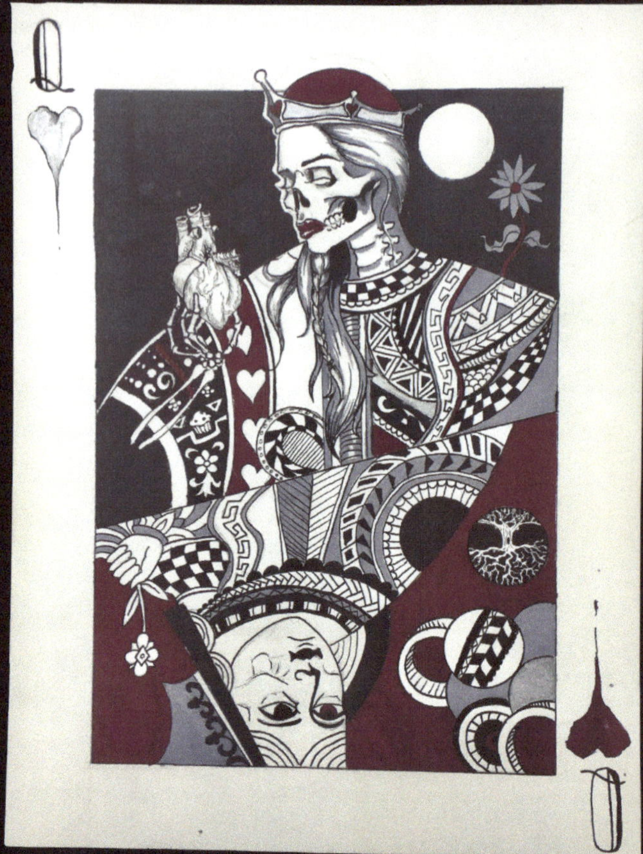

"Queen of Hearts"

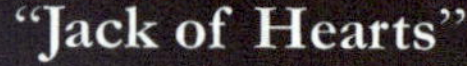

"Jack of Hearts"

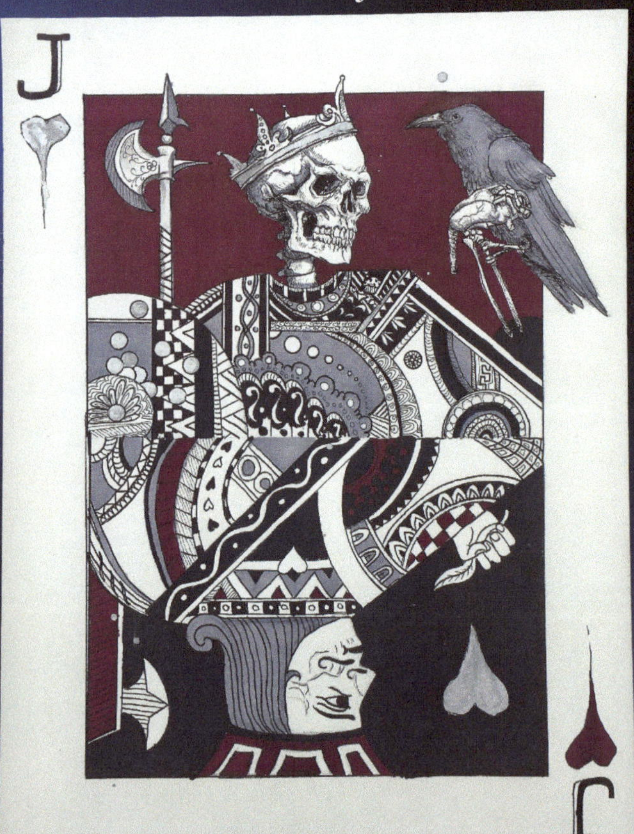

From the **Deck of Cards** Series
2019

Paper
Pencil, Pen, Felt Marker
12.0 L × 9.0 W Inches

"Ace of Hearts"

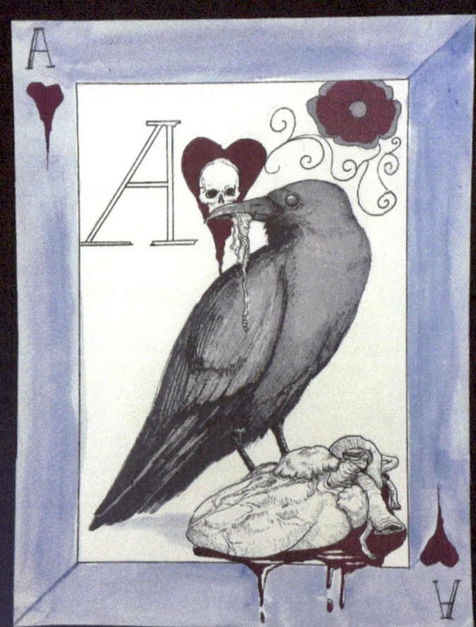

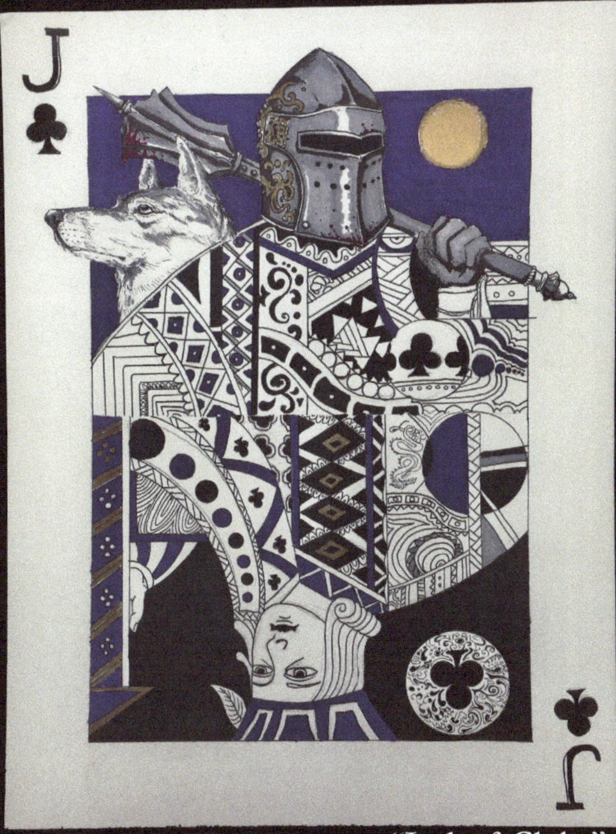

"Jack of Clubs"

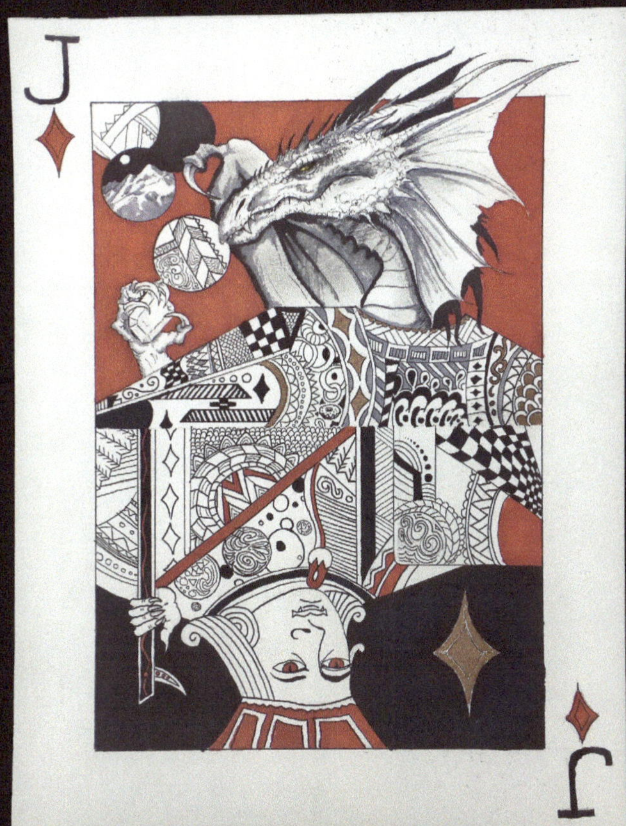

"Jack of Diamonds"

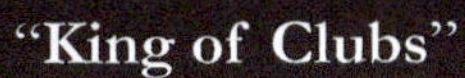

"King of Clubs"

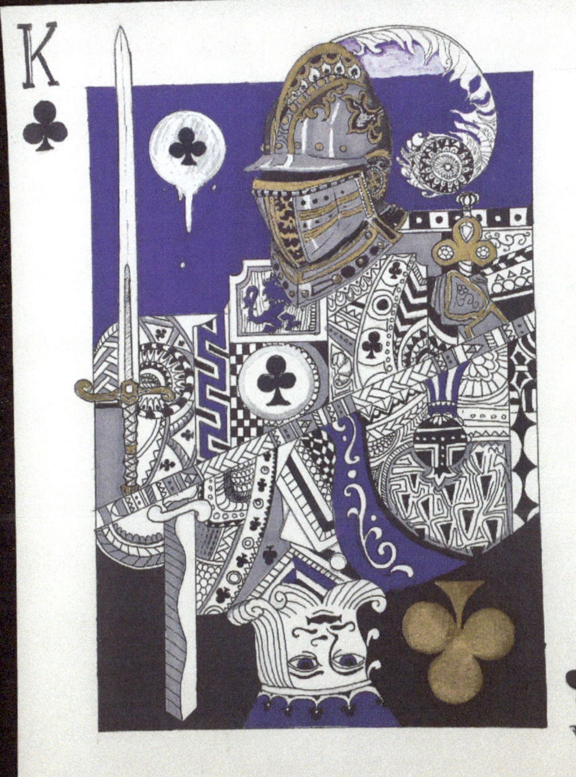

"King of Spades"

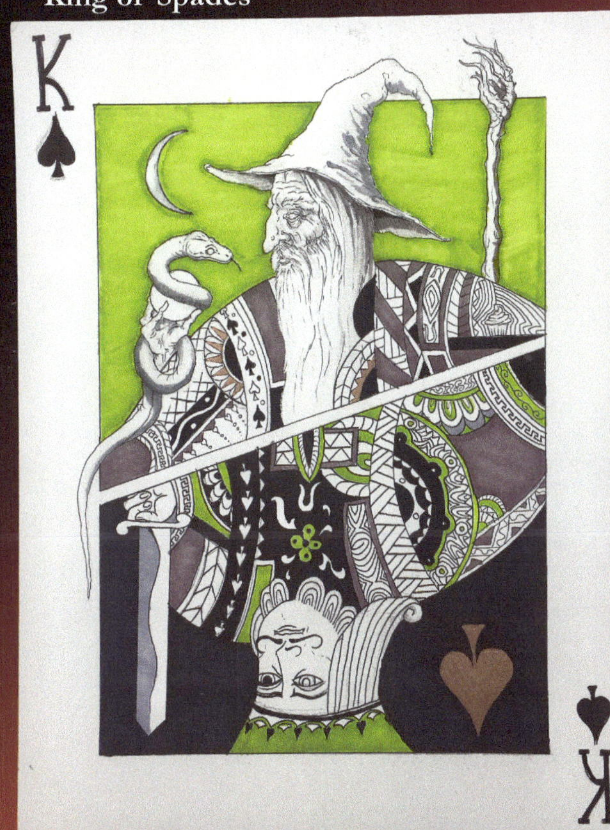

In the Archives of the
James William Christenson Art Gallery
Prior Lake, Minnesota

In the Archives of the
James William Christenson Art Gallery
Prior Lake, Minnesota

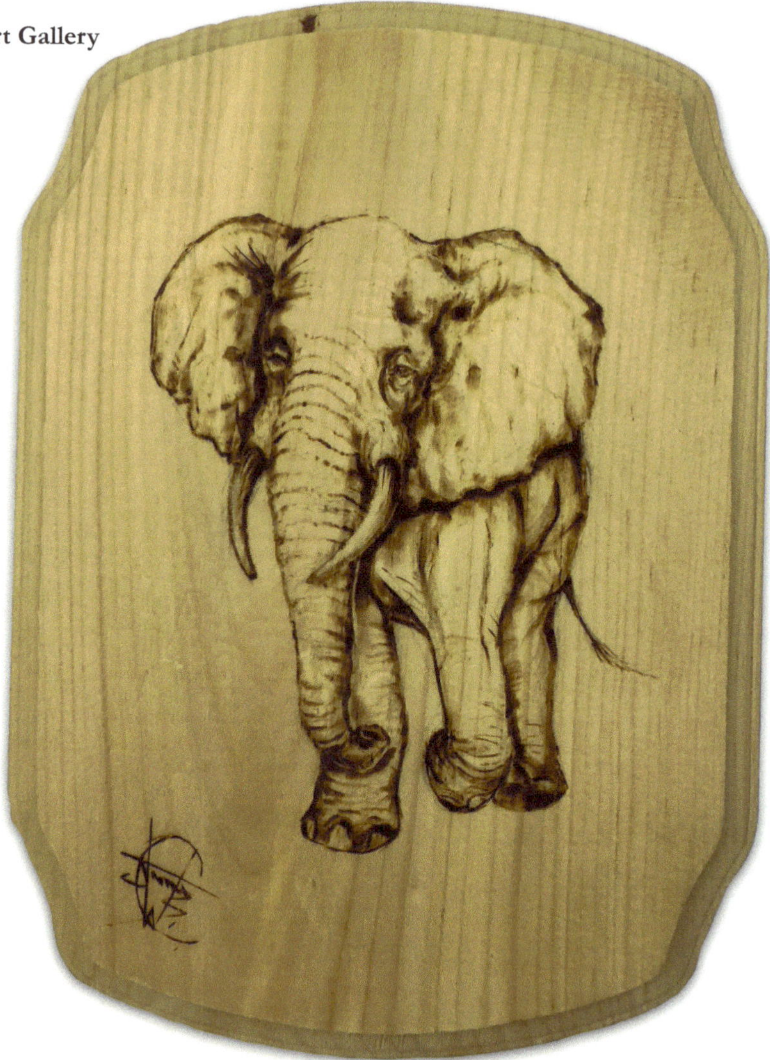

"Elephant"
2018

Unfinished Maple Plaque
Woodburn
9.5 L × 6.75 W Inches

"Maine Harbor"
2019

Unfinished Pine Coaster
Woodburn
4.0 L × 4.0 W Inches

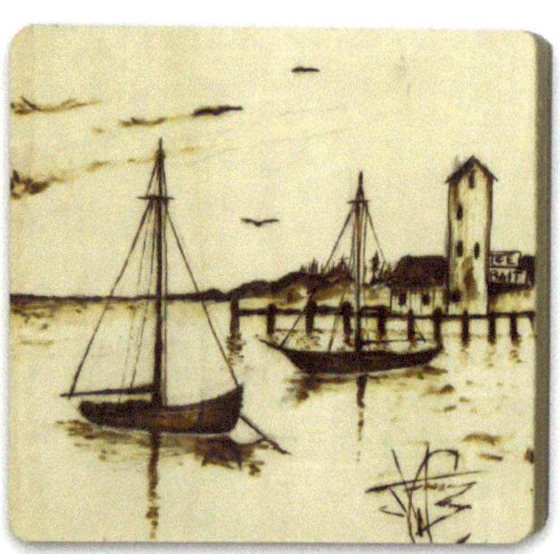

"Owl"
2019

Unfinished Pine Coaster
Woodburn
4.0 L × 4.0 W Inches

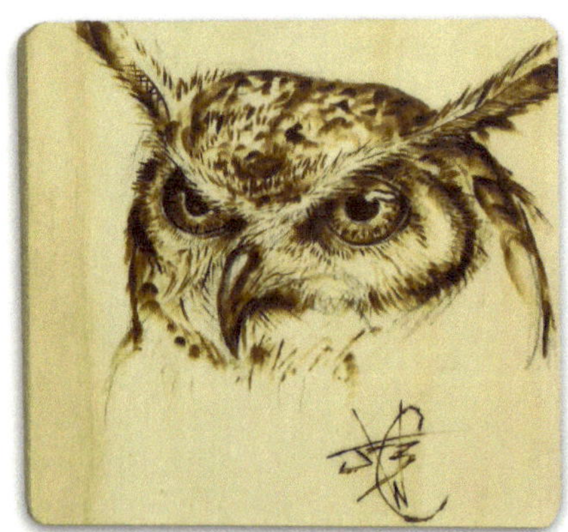

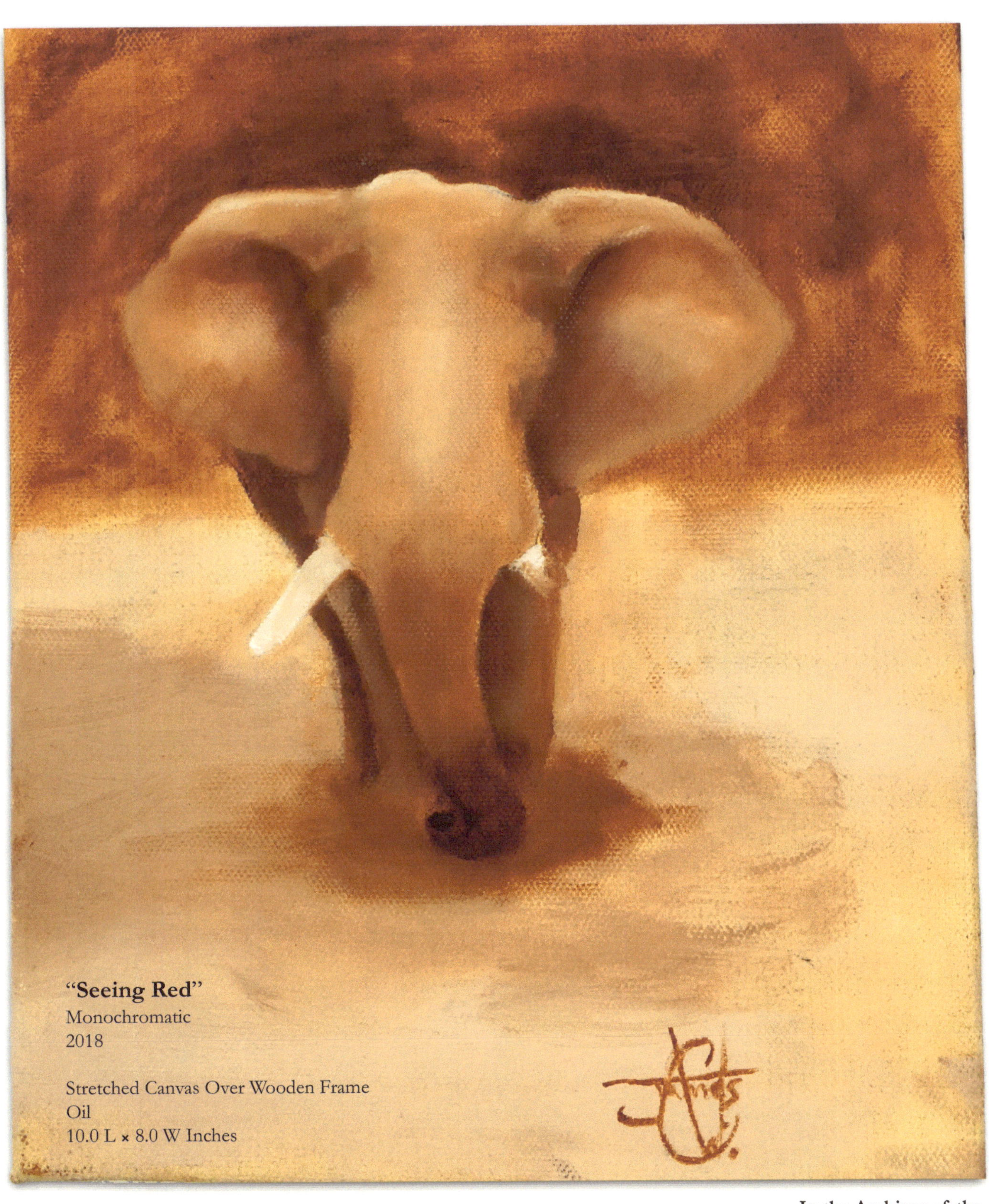

In the Archives of the
James William Christenson Art Gallery
Prior Lake, Minnesota

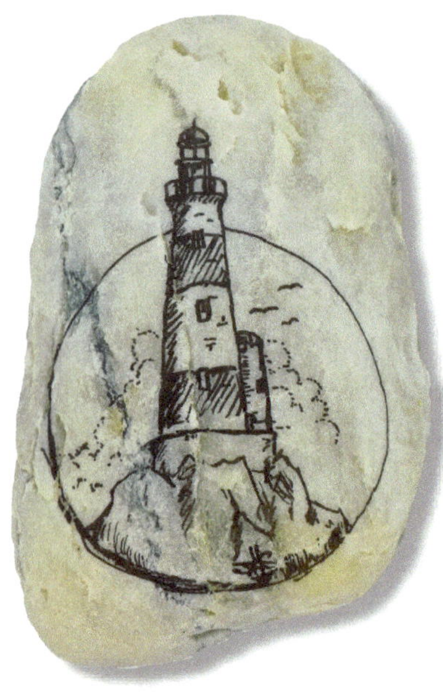

"Misty Withers"
Actual Size
2018

Milky Quartz
Ink
3.0 L × 2.0 W Inches

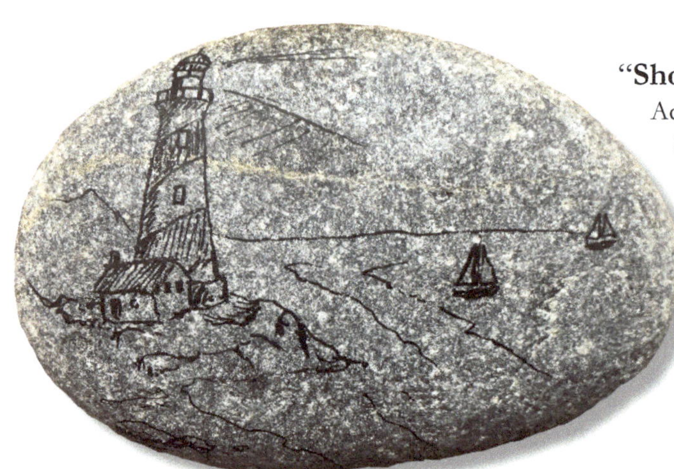

"Shores"
Actual Size
2018

Atlantic Ocean Seashore Rock
Ink
3.0 L × 2.0 W Inches

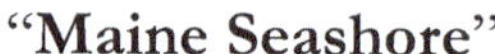

"Maine Seashore"
Actual Size
2018

Atlantic Ocean Seashore Rock
Ink
2.5 L × 2.0 W Inches

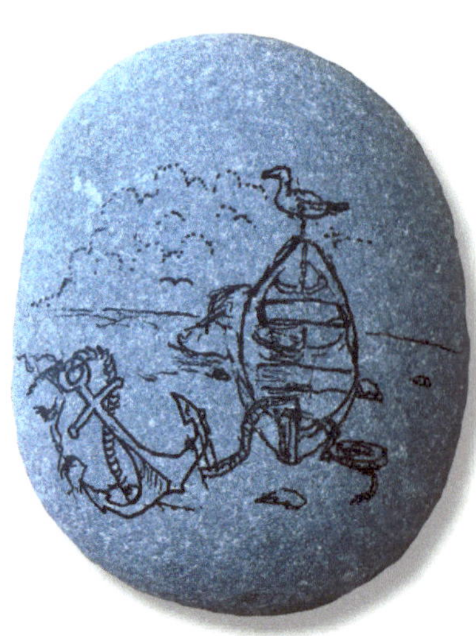

**In the Archives of the
James William Christenson Art Gallery
Prior Lake, Minnesota**

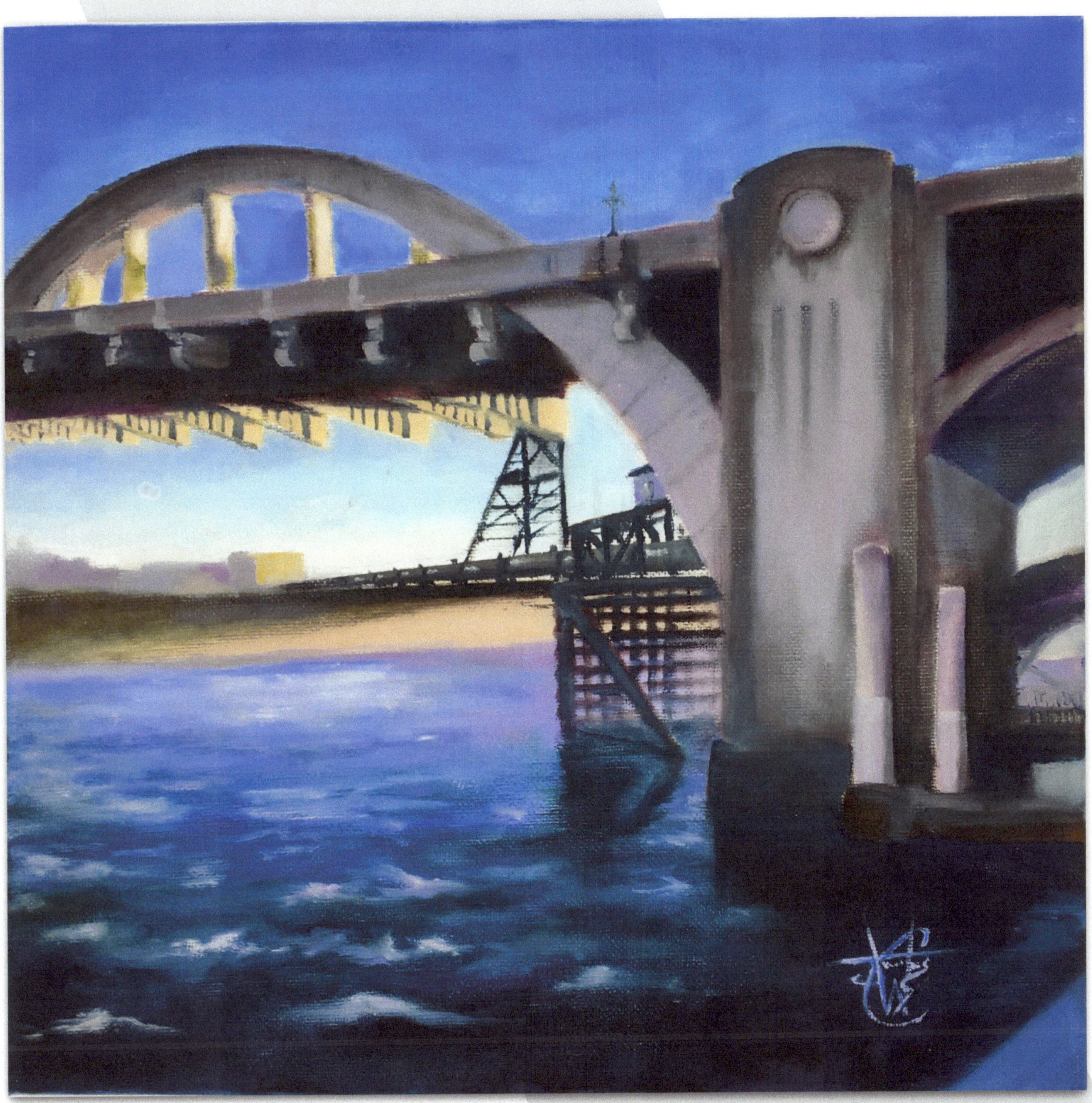

In the Archives of the
James William Christenson Art Gallery
Prior Lake, Minnesota

"Robert Street Bridge"
2018

Stretched Canvas Over Wooden Frame
Oil
12.0 L × 12.0 W Inches

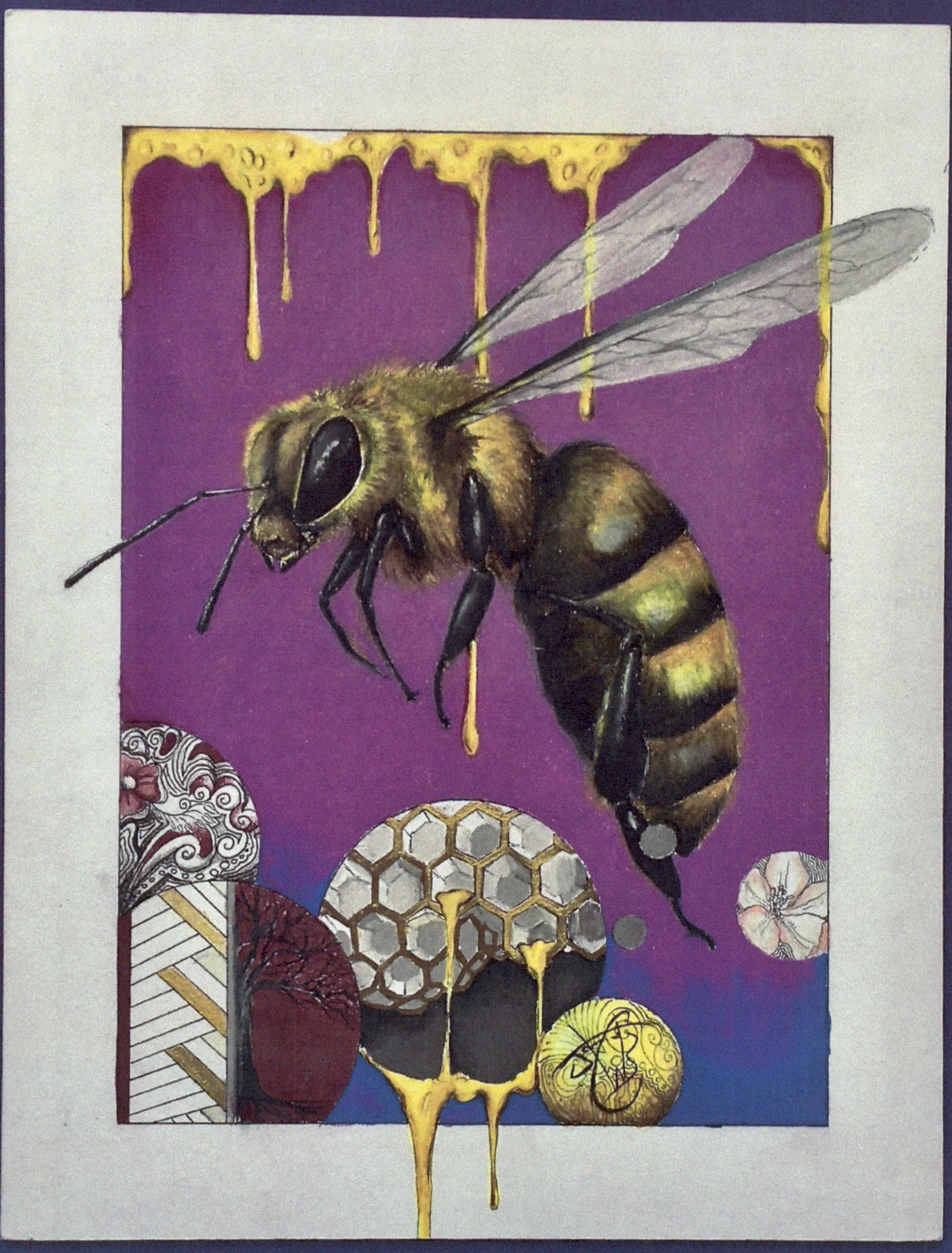

"A Sticky Situation"
2018

Paper
Colored Pencil, Ink
12.0 L × 8.5 W Inches

In the Archives of the
James William Christenson Art Gallery
Prior Lake, Minnesota

"Uncle Doug"
Character Sketch
2018

Paper
Pen, Pencil, Felt Marker
13.0 L × 9.5 W Inches

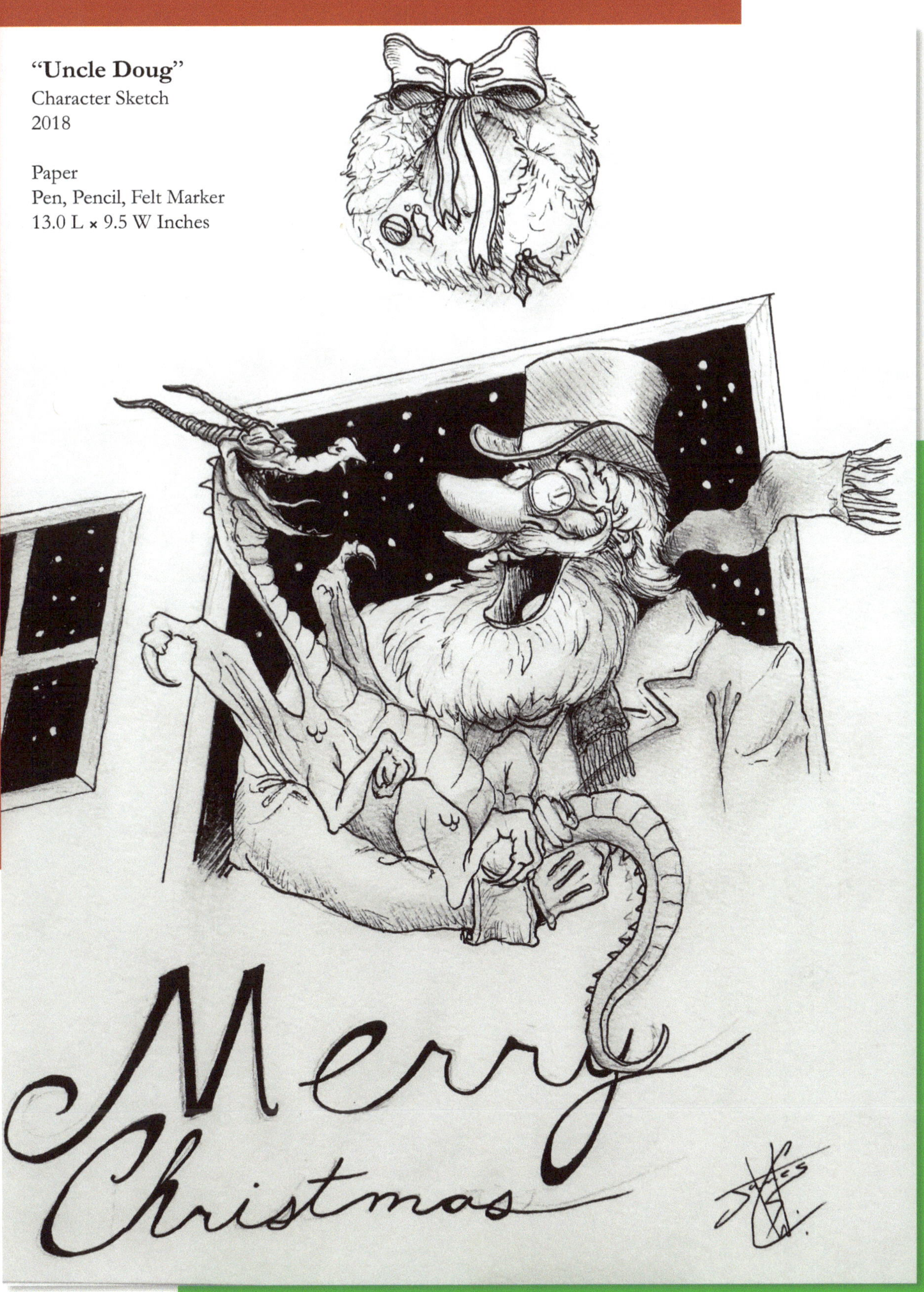

In the Archives of the
James William Christenson Art Gallery
Prior Lake, Minnesota

www.ingramcontent.com/pod-product-compliance
Lightning Source LLC
LaVergne TN
LVHW070157110826
845147LV00002B/429
9781732712997